GINO'S

ITALIAN COASTAL ESCAPE

GINO D'ACAMPO

First published in Great Britain in 2017 by Hodder
& Stoughton
An Hachette UK company

1

Copyright © ITV Ventures Ltd 2017

Recipes copyright © Gino D'Acampo 2017
Photography copyright © Dan Jones 2017

Additional photography copyright © Abbi-Rose Crook
4, 72, 98, 134, 169, 199; Gino D'Acampo 224;
Matt Russell 198; Shutterstock.com 26–27, 78–79,
110–11, 162–63

Television series *Gino's Italian Coastal Escape*
copyright © ITV Studios Limited 2017.
Licensed by ITV Ventures Ltd. All rights reserved.

Map © Louise Lockhart 2017
(The Printed Peanut)

A CIP catalogue record for this title is available from
the British Library

Hardback ISBN 978 1   73 661516
eBook ISBN 978 1 473 66152 3

Editorial Director: Nicky Ross
Project Editor: Polly Boyd
Assistant Editor: Lauren Whelan
Design and art direction: Georgia Vaux
Photography: Dan Jones
Food Stylist: Gee Charman
Props Stylist: Tonia Shuttleworth
Shoot Producer: Ruth Ferrier
Proofreader: Miren Lopategui
Indexer: Caroline Jones

Typeset in Univers
Colour origination by Born
Printed and bound in Germany by Mohn media

Hodder & Stoughton policy is to use papers that
are natural, renewable and recyclable products
and made from wood grown in sustainable forests.
The logging and manufacturing processes are expected
to conform to the environmental regulations of the
country of origin.

Hodder & Stoughton Ltd
Carmelite House
50 Victoria Embankment
London
EC4Y 0DZ

www.hodder.co.uk

GINO'S

ITALIAN COASTAL ESCAPE

A TASTE OF ITALY FROM THE AEOLIAN
ISLANDS TO ELBA

GINO D'ACAMPO

CONTENTS

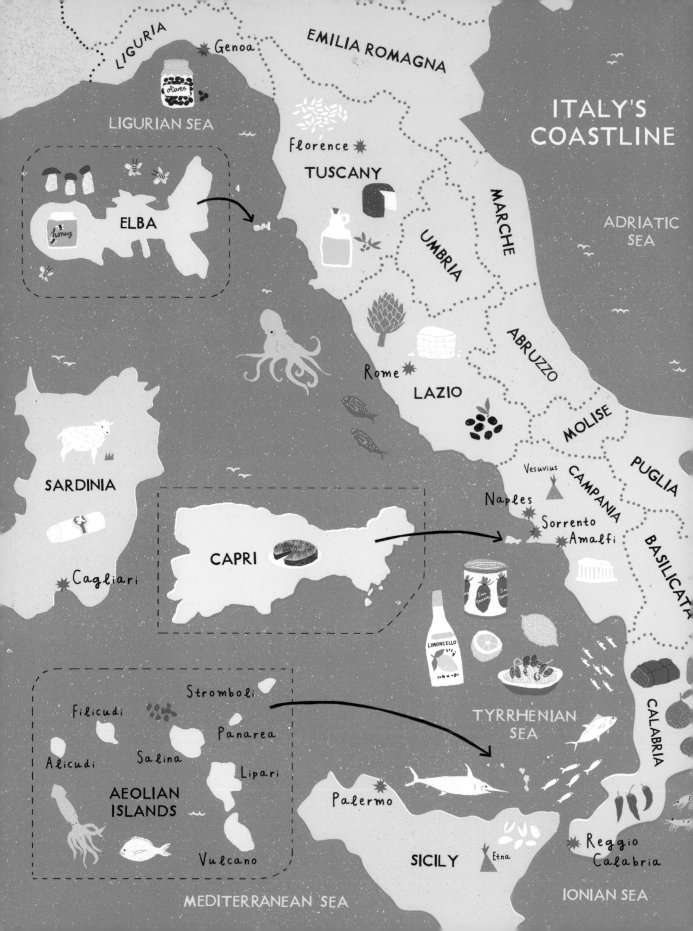

INTRODUCTION

On this latest journey to my wonderful homeland to film *Gino's Italian Coastal Escape* I travelled up Italy's west coast visiting the Aeolian Islands, Calabria, Campania, Capri, Lazio, Tuscany (*Toscana*) and Elba. It was an amazing trip in so many ways, and I was reminded once again of the beauty of the Italian coastline, the incredible quality of the ingredients, and how passionate the locals are about their food, especially their regional specialities.

THE AEOLIAN ISLANDS

I was particularly excited about visiting the Aeolian islands, as I'd heard so much about them yet had never been there before. Situated in the Tyrrhenian Sea, 25km northeast of Sicily (the jumping-off point for the ferry), the archipelago consists of seven tiny volcanic islands – Salina and Panarea (both of which we visited), Lipari, Vulcano, Stromboli, Filicudi and Alicudi. All are protected by UNESCO as a World Heritage Site.

Salina is remarkably green and lush because of its natural freshwater springs. As its name (which means 'salt mill' in Italian) implies, salt is a major part of this island's economy, but it is also famous for its delicious capers and exquisite sweet Malvasia wine. Panarea – the smallest and chicest of the islands – has a rocky, dramatic landscape and is inhabited on just one side. Cars aren't allowed, so residents drive around in three-wheel trucks, golf buggies and scooters. Since just about everything has to be shipped in, the ferry arrivals are a riotous affair as lorry loads of goods are stacked precariously onto these tiny, basic vehicles. The surrounding waters are full of fish, crustaceans and squid. I was lucky enough to go fishing off the island and was thrilled to catch one of the local specialities – *totano*, the red squid.

CALABRIA

We then travelled to the mainland, to the region of Calabria. If Sicily is considered the football of Italy, Calabria is the toe of the boot that's kicking it – and because there is only a thin sliver of water separating the two regions, their history is very similar. Calabria has one of the oldest records of human habitation in Italy, dating back to around 700,000 BCE. For some reason relatively few tourists visit Calabria (although numbers are increasing every year), but I really don't understand why – it's a natural paradise, with 485 miles of coastline and spectacular mountains, and it's still remarkably unspoilt.

Food traditions are very important in Calabria. Vegetables and fruit are widely cultivated, with highlights including Tropea onions, aubergines, figs, liquorice and bergamot, which is not grown anywhere else in Italy (see pages 26–27). One thing locals really know about is the art of preserving food – through salting, smoking, oiling and curing – to counteract spoilage that would otherwise occur rapidly in the humid climate. I love the fact that many local festivals (*sagre*) are held each year to honour the regional ingredients. I think Calabria is a very special place that still sees beauty in the simple things in life.

CAMPANIA & CAPRI

Moving up the boot I then travelled to Campania, which is where I grew up and my family still lives (and that includes 62 crazy cousins!). This wonderful region encompasses hills, mountains, fertile lowland plains and breathtakingly beautiful coastal areas, which give rise to a wonderfully varied cuisine that draws inspiration from both land and sea (see pages 78–79).

Campania is known as one of the poorer regions of Italy, and that may well be the case when it comes to the economy, but to me it's one of the richest in so many ways. The pace of life is slow, the food is outstanding and the people are warm and full of character. I know I'm biased because it's my home, but it really has so much to offer. You can sunbathe on a Sorrento beach, stroll down the cobbled streets of the picturesque cliffside village of Positano, wonder at the beauty and tragic destruction of Pompeii and Herculaneum almost two thousand years ago, feel the brooding presence of Mount Vesuvius – the only active volcano on mainland Europe – and experience the hustle and bustle of the vibrant city of Naples. Everything you could ever want from a holiday is to be found right there. I try not to be too gushing about this region, but I just love everything about it! And of course there is also the gorgeous neighbouring island of Capri, which is pure opulence with its designer shops and elite restaurants. The must-see site on Capri is the Blue Grotto, a dark cavern where the sea glows electric blue. It is truly magical.

If you ever visit Campania – which you really should if you can – you simply must try the buffalo mozzarella; what many of you know as mozzarella is just not the real thing. And the Neapolitan pizzas – wow … and the freshly caught seafood … and the ice cream … ahhhhhhhhh … OK, I'm getting carried away. Maybe I'd better move on to the next region …

LAZIO

My travels then took me to Lazio, in central Italy, home of the capital city of Rome. Of course, everyone loves to visit Rome – its history and architecture are phenomenal and there is so much to do there, but if you visit the city do try to build in more time so you can venture outside to experience the great pleasures that await you in the rest of this fascinating region. Of Lazio's 5.8 million inhabitants 4 million live in Rome, so you can see that once you leave the city you can certainly find plenty of peace and quiet in the surrounding areas. There are spectacular nature reserves, stunning lakes and wonderful old stone-built villages. The ancient coastal city of Gaeta, just over 100km south of Rome, is also a must. There you'll find the distinctive Gaeta olives and *tiella*, a delicious snack food, as well as many other local specialities (see pages 110–11).

The food in Lazio can be sophisticated or simple and down to earth. Generally, it is richer and more robustly flavoured than the cuisine of neighbouring regions. Braised meat and slow-cooked stews are popular, and appetising dishes are made out of traditional 'poor man's' ingredients such as offal. Some of the best-known pasta sauces originate in this region (including *carbonara* and *arrabbiata*), and the pasta itself tends to be thick and chunky. Other staples include *polenta* and *gnocchi*. Pulses and seafood are popular in the region, and fresh vegetables feature prominently in Lazio cuisine, as the fertile volcanic soil around Rome is ideal for their cultivation.

TUSCANY & ELBA

My final stop was Tuscany. This region, especially Florence, is regarded as the birthplace of the Renaissance, and art and fashion are still as important as ever. However, it also has a more rustic side, which I experienced when I spent an amazing day herding cattle with the famous Tuscan cowboys (*butteri*). The Tuscan style of cooking is generally fairly rustic too, and I love it. Locals seek out only the freshest seasonal produce, so incredible meals are created from whatever is at its best in the market that day. Although the cuisine can be regarded as basic, because it generally doesn't include lots of sauces or spices, the amazing quality of the raw ingredients (see pages 162–63) means that dishes are always full of flavour. White truffles are a special treat that appear in October and November in San Miniato, and the beef from the Chiana Valley is outstanding, so perfect for the popular local speciality *bistecca alla fiorentina* (Florentine steak). As well as tasting delicious, Tuscan food is hearty and filling, probably because bread (often unsalted) is served in or with most dishes. Tuscan wine is also excellent.

I must reserve a special mention for Elba – a stunning, quaint island 10km off the coast of Tuscany. It holds particularly fond memories for me, as it was where I spent my first-ever family holiday. As you may know, this is where Napoleon was exiled for nine months. Quite honestly, I don't know why he didn't just stay and enjoy the rest of his life here – it's hard to think of a better place to retire or be banished to! You're constantly reminded of Napoleon's presence on Elba, but funnily enough when I think of the island what comes to mind first is tasting a pizza made with chickpea flour. At first I was sceptical, but after tasting the pizza I was well and truly converted!

In this brief introduction I have tried to describe some of the wonderful places I was lucky enough to visit and have only touched on the exciting regional ingredients and specialities I discovered there, but you'll find plenty more information on these elsewhere in the book. I know that some of you may never visit Italy, but hopefully with these simple and delicious recipes, which were inspired by my recent trip, I can bring a little bit of Italy to you.

Buon appetito!

Gino xxx

Whenever I travel around Italy I can't resist trying out a wide range of new and different antipasti — for me, they're frequently the highlight of the meal. For this book I've chosen recipes that have a real 'wow' factor. They look and taste amazing, yet the ingredients are mostly easy to find and the dishes simple to prepare — I firmly believe 'special' doesn't have to mean complicated. If you're on the Italian coast you'll always find *antipasti di pesce* (seafood antipasti), so I've included a good selection of seafood recipes here, including tuna carpaccio (raw tuna), two fish salads, fritto misto (mixed fried seafood), a seafood gratin and a traditional fish soup. The other dishes feature meat, vegetables, cheese and even fruit. Generally, hot antipasti are served only before a light meal in Italy.

ANTIPASTI & SOUPS

SALT COD & POTATO SALAD WITH RED ONION & CAPERS

TUNA CARPACCIO WITH ROCKET, CAPERS & BALSAMIC

SEARED SALMON SALAD

BEEF CARPACCIO WITH HORSERADISH & PARMESAN CREAM SAUCE

BAKED PEACHES WITH PARMA HAM & BOCCONCINI MOZZARELLA

PEAR, DOLCELATTE & MASCARPONE TART WITH HONEY & THYME

RICE CROQUETTES WITH ARRABBIATA SAUCE

PRAWN & SCALLOP GRATIN

MIXED FRIED SEAFOOD WITH SPICY LEMON MAYONNAISE

CHICKEN LIVER SKEWERS WITH LEMON BUTTER SAUCE

CANNELLINI BEAN, RED LENTIL & CHILLI SOUP

ROASTED LEEK, CELERY & SPINACH SOUP

AMALFI-STYLE FISH SOUP

SALT COD & POTATO SALAD WITH RED ONION & CAPERS

INSALATONA DI BACCALÀ CON PATATE, CIPOLLE ROSSE E CAPPERI

Baccalà is cod that has been preserved in salt and then air-dried. In the days before refrigeration and good transport links it was preserved out of necessity, so those living inland could enjoy fish all year round. Today there is still a great demand for salt cod, even in coastal areas where fresh fish is abundant – in Calabria, which is surrounded by the sea, it is one of the most popular forms of seafood. It is less widely available in Britain, but you can usually find it in large supermarkets, Italian delis or online. Before cooking, always soak the fish in cold water for 48 hours to rehydrate it and remove excess salt.

450g salt cod, cut into 6 equal-sized pieces
500g Charlotte potatoes, scrubbed
1 large red onion, peeled and finely sliced
30g capers, drained
3 tablespoons chopped fresh flat-leaf parsley

For the dressing
60ml freshly squeezed lemon juice
2 garlic cloves, peeled and crushed
100ml extra virgin olive oil
Pinch of salt

Serves 6

1] To prepare the salt cod, rinse thoroughly under cold running water. Place in a large bowl and pour over cold water then cover with cling film and refrigerate. Leave to soak for 48 hours, changing the water often. Drain and rinse.

2] Place the fish in a medium saucepan with 2 litres of cold unsalted water. Bring to the boil then reduce the heat and simmer for 10 minutes. To test if the cod is done, pull back a small piece of flesh with a fork – it should flake easily. Drain and set aside to cool.

3] Put the potatoes in a medium saucepan and cover with cold unsalted water. Bring to the boil. Reduce the heat and simmer for 20 minutes or until the potatoes feel tender when pierced with a knife. Drain and set aside to cool.

4] To make the dressing, put the lemon juice and garlic in a small bowl and gradually whisk in the olive oil. Add the salt.

5] Place the onion, capers and parsley in a large bowl. Using a fork or your fingers, flake the cooled fish into the bowl, discarding any skin and bones.

6] Slice the cooled potatoes into rounds about 1cm thick and add to the bowl with the fish. Pour over the dressing and gently stir to combine. Transfer to a serving platter.

TUNA CARPACCIO WITH ROCKET, CAPERS & BALSAMIC

CARPACCIO DI TONNO CON RUCOLA, CAPPERI E BALSAMICO

This dish looks amazing and requires no cooking whatsoever, so it's perfect for when you're entertaining. To make life even easier, you can assemble it up to an hour ahead while you enjoy an *aperitivo* with your guests. The sweetness of the balsamic glaze and the saltiness of the capers is a combination made in heaven. It's vital to use very fresh, good-quality tuna for this dish. Serve with toasted ciabatta and a bottle of chilled sparkling wine such as Franciacorta.

Serves 4

300g tuna loin fillet
4 tablespoons extra virgin olive oil
60g rocket leaves
3 tablespoons nonpareille capers, drained

4 tablespoons balsamic glaze
Sea salt flakes
Freshly ground black pepper

1] Wrap the tuna tightly in cling film to create a cylindrical shape. Place in the freezer for about 3 hours until firm but not frozen hard. Put 4 flat serving plates in the fridge.

2] Remove the tuna from the freezer and discard the cling film. Place the fish on a board. Using a very sharp, long-bladed knife, cut across into very thin slices, about the same thickness as smoked salmon.

3] Arrange the tuna slices on the chilled plates. Drizzle over the oil and sprinkle over a few sea salt flakes and a little pepper.

4] Arrange the rocket along the top of the tuna and scatter over the capers. Drizzle over the balsamic glaze.

SEARED SALMON SALAD

INSALATA CON SALMONE SCOTTATO

Salmon is not native to southern Italy, but it often features on the menus of trendy establishments. The chefs like to get creative, combining the rich, oily fish with classic Italian flavours like olives, orange, lemon, fennel, tomatoes and extra virgin olive oil. In this recipe you can use rocket instead of spinach if you prefer, and feel free to add olives or capers for added depth of flavour. Serve with warm, crusty bread.

Serves 6

500g skinned salmon fillet
1 tablespoon extra virgin olive oil
350g frozen podded broad beans
350g baby spinach leaves
1 large fennel bulb, cored
Salt and freshly ground black pepper

For the dressing
Grated zest and juice of ½ unwaxed orange
1 teaspoon Dijon mustard
3 tablespoons extra virgin olive oil

1] Brush the salmon with the oil and season both sides with salt. Place a large frying pan over a medium to high heat. When hot, add the salmon and fry for 6 minutes, then turn and fry for a further 3 minutes. Set aside to cool.

2] Put the broad beans in a small pan and cover with water. Bring to the boil, cover and simmer for 3 minutes. Drain and rinse under cold running water then slip the beans out of their skins. Put in a medium bowl and add the spinach.

3] Slice the fennel very finely lengthways, either on a mandolin or using a sharp knife. Put in the bowl with the beans and spinach.

4] To make the dressing, combine the orange zest and juice and mustard in a small bowl. Gradually add the oil, whisking vigorously as you go, then season with salt and pepper.

5] Pour half the dressing over the vegetables and gently toss together. Transfer to a large serving platter.

6] Using a fork or your fingers, flake the cooled fish into large chunks and scatter them over the salad. Drizzle over the remaining dressing and season with salt and pepper.

BEEF CARPACCIO WITH HORSERADISH & PARMESAN CREAM SAUCE

CARPACCIO DI MANZO CON CREMINA AL PARMIGIANO E RAFANO

Beef carpaccio is one of those dishes that you tend to order in a restaurant, thinking you could never make it at home. It looks so impressive, yet it's actually incredibly simple. The slicing is the hardest part, but if you freeze the beef for 30 minutes first it will be a lot easier. The horseradish and Parmesan cream sauce in this recipe perfectly complement the raw beef. Serve with toasted ciabatta.

300g beef fillet (ideally the centre cut)
35g frisée lettuce
20g Parmesan cheese shavings

For the sauce
100ml double cream
1 teaspoon hot horseradish sauce
1 teaspoon white wine vinegar
1½ tablespoons freshly grated
  Parmesan cheese
Freshly ground black pepper

Serves 4

1] To make the sauce, put the cream, horseradish sauce, vinegar and Parmesan in a small bowl. Season with pepper and stir to combine. Cover with cling film and chill until ready to serve.

2] Using a sharp knife, slice the beef very thinly. Place a slice between two layers of cling film. Using a meat mallet or heavy-based pan, pound the meat as thinly as possible without tearing it. Repeat for all the slices. Arrange the beef on a large serving platter.

3] Pile the frisée lettuce on top of the beef, drizzle over the Parmesan and horseradish cream and scatter over the Parmesan shavings. Season with pepper.

BAKED PEACHES WITH PARMA HAM & BOCCONCINI MOZZARELLA

PESCHE AL FORNO CON PROSCIUTTO CRUDO E BOCCONCINI DI MOZZARELLA

Some of the best peaches are grown in Campania, in southern Italy. In season between June and September, the most widely available are the yellow peach (*pesca gialla*) and the white peach (*pesca bianca*), although many other more unusual varieties are grown on a smaller scale. Roasted peaches were enjoyed in the Roman times, and although they're usually eaten as a dessert today they also work wonderfully in savoury dishes, as in this recipe – the flavour and texture combinations of the sweet, soft fruit with the salty, crisp ham and tangy, smooth mozzarella are sensational. If you prefer, use roasted figs instead of peaches.

Serves 4

4 ripe peaches, halved and stone removed
3 tablespoons extra virgin olive oil
3 tablespoons balsamic glaze
8 large slices of Parma ham
4 slices of ciabatta bread, about 1cm thick

1 garlic clove, peeled
300g bocconcini mozzarella cheese (mini mozzarella, mozzarella pearls), drained
60g rocket leaves
Salt and freshly ground black pepper

1] Preheat the oven to 180°C/gas mark 4. Put the peaches, cut-side up, on a baking sheet. Drizzle over 1 tablespoon each of the oil and balsamic glaze. Season with salt and pepper. Roast for about 20 minutes or until soft (the cooking time depends on ripeness). Remove from the oven and set aside.

2] Arrange the ham on a non-stick baking sheet, about 30 x 38cm. Lay a piece of foil on top then place a smaller baking sheet, about 25 x 35cm, on top of the foil. Bake for 5 minutes or until the ham is very crisp. Remove the top baking sheet and foil. Leave to cool.

3] Toast the ciabatta on both sides until golden and rub all over with the garlic. Drizzle the remaining 2 tablespoons of oil over the toasted side.

4] Divide the bocconcini, rocket, peaches and ham among 4 serving plates. Drizzle over the remaining 2 tablespoons of balsamic glaze and season with salt and pepper. Serve with the toasted ciabatta.

PEAR, DOLCELATTE & MASCARPONE TART
WITH HONEY & THYME

TORTA DI PERE, DOLCELATTE E MASCARPONE CON MIELE E TIMO

I know that buying shop-bought pastry is cheating, but making puff pastry from scratch is a bit of a faff. And besides, with the shop-bought variety this dish can be prepared in about 15 minutes – and if that's what it takes to get you into the kitchen, I've won! The combination of honey and cheese is very popular in Italy, the sweetness of honey contrasting particularly well with cheeses that are mild and creamy (ricotta), salty (pecorino) or sharp (aged blue cheeses). Serve with a crisp, mixed-leaf salad dressed with extra virgin olive oil and balsamic vinegar.

Serves 6

2 conference pears
Plain flour for dusting
320g shop-bought puff pastry
150g Dolcelatte cheese (room temperature)
150g mascarpone cheese (room temperature)
1 medium egg, lightly beaten

15g pine nuts
1 tablespoon fresh thyme leaves
2 tablespoons runny honey
Freshly ground black pepper

1] Preheat the oven to 180°C/gas mark 4. Peel the pears, slice in half through the stem and remove the core. Cut lengthways into slices about 5mm thick. Set aside.

2] Line a baking sheet, about 30 x 38cm, with baking parchment. Lightly dust the work surface with flour. Roll out the pastry into a rectangle slightly smaller than the baking sheet and carefully transfer the pastry to the prepared sheet.

3] Combine the Dolcelatte and mascarpone in a small bowl. Spread the mixture onto the pastry, leaving a border of about 1cm around the edge.

4] Arrange the pears in slightly overlapping rows on top of the cheese mixture and brush the border with the egg. Bake for 15 minutes.

5] Remove from the oven and scatter over the pine nuts and thyme. Return to the oven for a further 5 minutes or until golden. Drizzle over the honey and season with black pepper. Serve warm.

CALABRIAN SPECIALITIES

The southernmost region of mainland Italy, Calabria is the 'toe' to Italy's 'boot'. A narrow strip of land, it is surrounded by sea on three sides and contains some of the highest mountains in the country. Although Calabria is one of the poorest regions in Italy, it has a strong culinary tradition and many wonderful ingredients, some of which are found nowhere else. As in neighbouring Sicily, the food in Calabria is strongly influenced by Arabic cuisine and is often extremely spicy.

PEPERONCINO CALABRESE

The hot red Calabrian chilli *peperoncino calabrese* (see below), grown by almost every household in Calabria, is used to add flavour and heat to any number of dishes, from vegetable sauces and pork *ragù* for pasta to the local delicacy *nduja* (see opposite). No Calabrian meal is complete without these chilli peppers, used fresh, dried, whole or crushed.

AUBERGINES

Vegetables are very widely cultivated in Calabria, particularly aubergines, which were introduced to the Mediterranean by the Arabs when they ruled in the 9th and 10th centuries. They are incredibly popular in the region and are used in a great number of dishes in many ways, including fried, stewed, stuffed, baked or in pâté. One speciality is *ciambotta*, a stewed aubergine recipe that can be eaten hot or cold – it's a delicious must-try.

CAPERS

The Aeolian island of Salina, west of Calabria, is well known for its delicious capers, which thrive in the volcanic soil. They're used in many dishes in the region, in salads and in cooking, and they're sometimes served simply on their own with fresh home-made bread.

TROPEA ONIONS

Calabria is famous for its sweet red onions (*cipolle di Tropea*), which are in season in spring and summer. They're grown around Tropea, in the Vibo Valentia province of Calabria, on the cliffs that lead down to the sea. The bulbs, which vary in shape from round or oval to elongated, are a wonderful deep purple colour. These onions are a chef's favourite, and are either served raw in salads or are used in cooking.

BERGAMOT

Almost a quarter of Italy's citrus fruit is grown in Calabria, including bergamot (see below), which is not cultivated anywhere else in the country. About the size of an orange but greenish yellow in colour, and more bitter-tasting, the pulp is used in marmalade, and the essential oil extracted from the peel is used to flavour Earl Grey tea and in the perfume industry. It is cultivated mainly along a small stretch of land in southern Calabria, where the temperature and soil are ideal. I've included a dessert flavoured with bergamot in this book (see page 196).

FIGS

Calabria is the principal fig-growing region in Italy. Abundant in September, this wonderful fruit is eaten raw or roasted and many are dried. Calabrian green 'Dottato' figs are considered the best in Italy, having smaller seeds and thicker skins than other figs, making them particularly juicy. A great Calabrian delicacy is figs stuffed with candied orange peel and nuts and dipped in chocolate (see pages 202–3).

FISH & FISH PRODUCTS

The seas around Calabria are rich in fish, particularly swordfish, tuna, sardines and anchovies. A local speciality is *mustica* (also known as *rosamarina*), often referred to as 'caviar for the poor'. It is made from newly hatched anchovies (*bianchetti*), which are salted, dried and then preserved in chilli-flavoured oil.

NDUJA

One of the most exciting ingredients in Calabrian cuisine is *nduja* (pronounced 'en-doo-zha', see below) – a spicy, spreadable sausage, or paste, made from pork and flavoured with hot red Calabrian chillies, which give it its rich red colour. It is usually spread on bread or toast, on its own or with cheese. It goes very well with seafood (see page 74) and transforms dishes by giving added fire – add a spoonful to pep up a sauce, stew or pizza. *Nduja* is made mainly in the town of Spilinga, in Vibo Valentia province, which is where it originated.

PORK & PORK PRODUCTS

Pork is by far the most popular meat in Calabria. Traditional breeds raised in the region are particularly large in size and well suited to the mountainous terrain and climate. Many pork products are produced there, including *prosciutto*, *pancetta*, *capocollo di Calabria* and salami, such as *soppressata*.

PITTA CALABRESE

Not to be confused with Middle-eastern pitta, *pitta calabrese* is a key part of the Calabrian diet. A round flatbread, often with a hole in the centre, it is stuffed and seasoned with various ingredients, including peppers, tomatoes, herbs, anchovies and *nduja*.

LIQUORICE

The climate and soil in Calabria are ideal for growing liquorice, particularly on the Ionian coast. Liquorice root (see below) is thought to aid digestion and is used in many dishes (see page 210). The Calabrians are so passionate about this plant that they have even built a museum dedicated to it, in Rossano.

SWEETS & CAKES

As in neighbouring Sicily, cakes and sweets are great delicacies in Calabria and are often infused with Middle-Eastern flavours. They are frequently linked to local traditions and festivals, such as Christmas, Easter and carnival time. *Mostaccioli*, made of honey, almonds and sweet wine, and *torrone di Bagnara*, a kind of nougat, are among the best known.

RICE CROQUETTES WITH ARRABBIATA SAUCE

ARANCINE ALL'ARRABBIATA

This is a Sicilian recipe I've given a Neapolitan twist by using buffalo mozzarella. You can prepare the croquettes a day ahead; just take them out of the fridge 30 minutes before you need them and roll them in the breadcrumbs once more before frying. The sauce can also be prepared ahead and reheated.

Makes 6

Saffron risotto (see page 147, except omit the peas)
200g '00' grade pasta flour
100g frozen peas, defrosted
2 x 125g balls of buffalo mozzarella cheese, drained and cut into small pieces
150g dried fine breadcrumbs
About 1 litre sunflower oil for deep-frying
Freshly ground black pepper

For the sauce
4 tablespoons extra virgin olive oil
2 garlic cloves, peeled and finely chopped
2 fresh, medium-hot red chillies, deseeded and finely sliced
2 x 400g tins of chopped tomatoes
3 tablespoons chopped fresh flat-leaf parsley
Salt

1] First make the sauce. Heat the oil in a large frying pan over a medium heat. Add the garlic and chillies and fry for about 1 minute, stirring continuously. Tip in the tomatoes and parsley and simmer gently for about 15 minutes, stirring occasionally. Season with salt and set aside.

2] Now make Saffron risotto (see page 147, except omit the peas). Cover and leave to cool for 15 minutes.

3] Meanwhile prepare the batter. Put the flour in a large bowl and add 300ml cold water gradually, whisking until smooth and very runny. Set aside.

4] Tip the cooled risotto onto a clean surface. Work the risotto in your hands for about 5 minutes, squeezing it to make it more compact (it helps if your hands are slightly damp). Shape into 6 balls. Place each ball in the palm of your hand and flatten it a little. Place some peas and mozzarella in the hollow part and gently close the rice around the filling. Dip each ball in the batter then roll lightly in the breadcrumbs to coat.

5] Heat a deep-fat fryer to 190°C, or heat the sunflower oil in a deep pan or wok until very hot. To test the temperature, add a small piece of bread; it will sizzle when the oil is hot enough for frying. Fry the rice balls in 2 batches for about 8 minutes or until golden brown. Remove with a slotted spoon and drain on kitchen paper. Gently heat the sauce and serve with the croquettes.

PRAWN & SCALLOP GRATIN

GAMBERONI E CAPESANTE GRATINATI

The Pozzuoli fish market in Campania is a real institution, both for the professional chef and domestic cook, so when I was in the area I couldn't resist stopping to buy some prawns and scallops to make this heavenly concoction. You can either make this in one large dish to share, as here, or in 4 individual gratin dishes, about 10 x 10cm. Serve with crusty bread to mop up the delicious garlicky sauce.

60g white bread (about 2 slices), crusts romovod

16 raw king prawns (about 160g), peeled and deveined

12 fresh red cherry tomatoes, quartered

8 extra-large scallops (about 200g), with corals attached if possible

130g salted butter (room temperature)

2 tablespoons chopped fresh flat-leaf parsley

1 garlic clove, peeled and crushed

½ teaspoon chilli powder

Grated zest of ½ unwaxed lemon

Salt

Serves 4

1] Preheat the oven to 150°C/gas mark 2. First make the dried breadcrumbs: cut the bread into 1cm cubes and spread on a baking sheet in a single layer. Bake for about 20 minutes until crisp and dry. Remove from the oven and leave to cool a little. Put the dried bread in a plastic food bag, seal the bag and crush with a rolling pin. Set aside.

2] Increase the oven temperature to 200°C/gas mark 6. Butterfly the prawns: place a prawn on its back and make a cut down the centre, but do not cut right through. Ease open with your thumb. Place the prawns in a baking dish, about 28 x 20cm.

3] Scatter the tomatoes over the prawns. Cut the scallops in half lengthways and arrange on top of the tomatoes.

4] Place the butter in a small bowl with the parsley, garlic, chilli powder and lemon zest and combine using the back of a fork, then season with salt. Stir in the dried breadcrumbs. Spread the buttery crumbs evenly over the scallops.

5] Bake for 10 minutes or until the breadcrumbs are golden. Serve immediately.

MIXED FRIED SEAFOOD WITH SPICY LEMON MAYONNAISE

FRITTO MISTO CON MAIONESE PICCANTE AL LIMONE

You will find fritto misto in every restaurant along Italy's Mediterranean coast. The classic ingredients are large prawns, anchovies, squid, sardines and sometimes whitebait, but the beauty of the dish is that you can use whatever is on offer at your fishmonger's. The coating is simple – just polenta, flour and seasoning – no egg, no milk, no water. You then just coat the fish, deep-fry and *ecco qua* – Italy's answer to fish and chips!

Serves 4

2 whole medium squid, about 200g in total
8 fresh whole anchovies, descaled and gutted
4 fresh whole sardines, descaled and gutted
4 large raw king prawns (head and shell on)
150g fine polenta
150g plain flour
1 litre sunflower oil for deep-frying

1 unwaxed lemon, cut into wedges
Salt and freshly ground black pepper

For the spicy lemon mayonnaise
250g good-quality mayonnaise
1½ teaspoons chilli powder
Juice of ½ lemon

1] To prepare the squid, pull the tentacles from the body. Feel inside the body and remove and discard the 'quill' (a transparent sliver of cartilage). Wash the inside of the body and peel off the outer skin. Cut off the squid tentacles just below the eyes (discard the head and guts). Discard the small, hard beak at the base of the tentacles. Rinse the tentacles and squid body in cold water.

2] Cut open the body pouch of each squid along one side and score the inner side with the tip of a small sharp knife into a fine diamond pattern. Cut each pouch into quarters (lengthways then across) and the tentacles in half. Rinse the anchovies, sardines and prawns.

3] Put the polenta and flour in a large shallow dish or roasting tin, season generously with salt and pepper and mix thoroughly. Carefully coat the squid, anchovies, sardines and prawns in the seasoned mix.

4] Heat a deep-fat fryer to 180°C or heat the oil in a deep pan or a wok until very hot. To test the temperature, drop a pinch of the flour mixture into the oil; it will sizzle when the oil is hot enough for frying.

5] Deep-fry the seafood in batches until golden and crisp, cooking the anchovies, sardines and prawns for about 1 minute and the squid for about 30 seconds. Remove with a slotted spoon and drain on kitchen paper. Meanwhile, combine all the ingredients for the spicy lemon mayonnaise in a small bowl. Serve the fried seafood immediately with the mayonnaise and lemon wedges.

CHICKEN LIVER SKEWERS WITH LEMON BUTTER SAUCE

SPIEDINI DI FEGATO DI POLLO CON SALSETTA AL BURRO E LIMONE

Every celebratory meal in Tuscany starts with chicken liver pâté, but personally I prefer the more robust simplicity of grilled, skewered chicken livers – silky smooth on the inside, with just a hint of crispness on the outside. I usually pop these skewers on the barbecue when I'm in Italy, but in the absence of a sunny day in Britain a kitchen grill will do the job. Make sure that you don't overcook the livers: they should be pink in the middle; if you cook them until they're browned all the way through, they will be dry and crumbly. Serve with a simple salad.

Serves 4

750g chicken livers, trimmed
2 tablespoons extra virgin olive oil
75g salted butter

Juice of 2 lemons
2 tablespoons chopped fresh flat-leaf parsley
Salt and freshly ground black pepper

1] Soak 4 wooden skewers, about 25cm long, in cold water for 30 minutes. Preheat the grill to its highest setting.

2] Thread the skewers with the chicken livers and place them on a large baking tray. Brush all over with the oil and season with salt and pepper. Grill the skewers for about 6 minutes, turning halfway through.

3] Meanwhile, heat the butter and lemon juice in a small saucepan over a low heat. As soon as the butter starts to melt, stir in the parsley.

4] Transfer the skewers to a serving plate and drizzle over the lemon butter.

CANNELLINI BEAN, RED LENTIL & CHILLI SOUP

ZUPPA PICCANTE DI CANNELLINI E LENTICCHIE ROSSE

This was cooked and served to me by my niece, Sara, when I visited her at her college near Viareggio, in Tuscany. If I'm honest, I wasn't expecting much, but I was really impressed by this spicy soup made from inexpensive ingredients. The Tuscans love their bean soups and generally use a lot of cannellini beans in their dishes – white, rich and creamy, they are incredibly versatile and healthy, being high in fibre, protein and antioxidants, and low in fat.

6 tablespoons extra virgin olive oil
1 large red onion, peeled and roughly chopped
2 large carrots, peeled and roughly chopped
2 celery sticks, roughly chopped
2 tablespoons tomato purée
1 teaspoon chilli powder

2 x 400g tins of cannellini beans, rinsed
  and drained
75g red split lentils, rinsed and drained
1 litre hot vegetable stock
Pinch of dried chilli flakes to garnish
A few parsley leaves to garnish

Serves 4

1] Heat 3 tablespoons of the oil in a medium saucepan over a medium heat. Add the onion, carrots and celery and fry for 15 minutes until softened but not browned, stirring occasionally. Stir in the tomato purée and chilli powder.

2] Add the beans (reserve 4 tablespoons for garnish), lentils and stock. Bring to the boil then reduce the heat, half-cover the pan and simmer for 20 minutes, stirring occasionally.

3] Remove the saucepan from the heat and purée using an electric blender or food processor until smooth. Check for seasoning.

4] To serve, ladle the soup into warm bowls and garnish with the reserved beans, the chilli flakes and parsley. Drizzle over the remaining 3 tablespoons of oil.

ROASTED LEEK, CELERY & SPINACH SOUP

ZUPPA DI PORRI AL FORNO, SEDANO E SPINACI

The depth of flavour in this soup is incredible, not to mention its rich, vibrant colour. Roasting and charring the leeks rather than simply frying them gives a lovely sweet, smoky flavour, while the mascarpone provides a hint of creaminess. I've used vegetable stock in this recipe, so it's suitable for vegetarians, but chicken stock would be fine too. Serve with warm crusty bread.

Serves 6

5 leeks, cut into rounds 3cm thick
6 tablespoons extra virgin olive oil
1 tablespoon fresh thyme leaves
1 large onion, peeled and roughly chopped
5 celery sticks, roughly chopped
150ml dry white wine

1.3 litres hot vegetable stock
250g fresh spinach
100g mascarpone cheese
15g toasted pine nuts
Salt and freshly ground black pepper

1] Preheat the oven to 200°C/gas mark 6. Place the leeks in a shallow roasting tin, about 25 x 35cm. Drizzle over 3 tablespoons of the oil, scatter over the thyme and season with salt and pepper. Use your hands to mix everything together thoroughly. Roast for 25 minutes, stirring halfway through. Remove from the oven and set aside.

2] Heat the remaining 3 tablespoons of oil in a medium saucepan over a medium heat. Add the onion and fry for 5 minutes, stirring occasionally. Add the celery and fry for about 3 minutes.

3] Increase the heat to high. Pour in the wine, bring to the boil and let it bubble for 1–2 minutes. Add the roasted leeks and the stock and bring to the boil. Reduce the heat to low and simmer gently for 20 minutes, stirring occasionally.

4] Stir in the spinach. When it has wilted (this will take a few seconds), remove the pan from the heat. Blend and season with salt and pepper.

5] To serve, ladle the soup into warm bowls. Add a spoonful of mascarpone in the centre and scatter over the pine nuts.

AMALFI-STYLE FISH SOUP

ZUPPA DI PESCE ALL'AMALFITANA

You can find wonderful fish soups and stews along the Amalfi coast. They all tend to be hearty, substantial and big on flavour, but there are many variations on the theme, depending on the cook's preference and what's available in the market on the day. Here I've used a mixture of haddock, red mullet and prawns, but plenty of other types of fish, as well as mussels, squid and clams, are also popular. Serve with plenty of fresh crusty bread to dunk in the liquid.

3 tablespoons extra virgin olive oil
1 large red onion, peeled and finely chopped
1 teaspoon dried chilli flakes
200ml dry white wine
400ml hot fish stock
1 x 400g tin of cherry tomatoes
300g skinless haddock fillet, cut into
  2cm chunks
300g skinless red mullet fillet, cut into
  2cm chunks

20 large raw prawns, peeled and deveined
1 x 400g tin of cannellini beans, rinsed
  and drained
10 fresh yellow cherry tomatoes, halved
4 tablespoons chopped fresh flat-leaf parsley
Grated zest of 1 unwaxed lemon
Salt

Serves 4

1] Heat the oil in a medium saucepan over a medium heat. Add the onion and chilli flakes and fry for 5 minutes, stirring occasionally.

2] Increase the heat to high. Pour in the wine, bring to the boil and let it bubble for 2 minutes. Stir in the stock and tinned cherry tomatoes, season with salt and bring to the boil. Reduce the heat to medium. Simmer for 20 minutes, stirring occasionally.

3] Reduce the heat and add the fish, prawns and beans. Simmer gently for 10 minutes, stirring occasionally.

4] Stir in the fresh cherry tomatoes and parsley and heat gently. Transfer to warm bowls and sprinkle over some lemon zest. Serve immediately.

I can't tell you how many times I've been asked for suggestions for romantic Italian meals for two. So for those who have asked, and for those who would like to know, this chapter is for you. I've included sumptuous dishes for special occasions, such as lobster and oysters, as well as less extravagant, 'cosier' meals, including a frittatina (Italian-style omelette) and the ultimate baked potato stuffed with Taleggio cheese. Of course, these dishes aren't only suitable for lovers — they're also ideal for that perfect evening in with a friend.

ITALIAN FOR TWO

AUBERGINE, MOZZARELLA & ROASTED RED PEPPER STACK

ITALIAN-STYLE SMOKED HADDOCK & PAPRIKA OMELETTE

DEEP-FRIED SPICY OYSTERS WITH BALSAMIC DIPPING SAUCE

SALMON ESCALOPES WITH CREAMY VERMOUTH SAUCE

SORRENTO-STYLE LOBSTER WITH LIMONCELLO & ROCKET

CHICKEN ESCALOPES WITH WILD MUSHROOMS & THYME

TWICE-BAKED JACKET POTATOES WITH LEEKS & TALEGGIO

SLICED RIB-EYE STEAK WITH BLACK PEPPER BUTTER

AUBERGINE, MOZZARELLA & ROASTED RED PEPPER STACK

TORRETTA DI MELANZANE, MOZZARELLA E PEPERONI ROSSI ARROSTITI

When I was filming *Gino's Italian Coastal Escape* I visited Paestum, near Salerno – home to three amazingly well-preserved ancient Greek temples dating back to 600 BCE. I also visited a local farm, where I lost my heart to Ana Maria – a lovely water buffalo whose milk is used to make the most exquisite buffalo mozzarella, a speciality of Campania (see page 78). There I prepared this super-simple but impressive dish, ideal for a first course or a light lunch. Serve with toasted ciabatta.

2 tablespoons chopped fresh flat-leaf parsley
1 tablespoon shredded fresh mint
125ml extra virgin olive oil
¾ teaspoon smoked paprika
Small handful of walnut halves
1 large aubergine

1 x 125g ball of buffalo mozzarella cheese, drained
50g Parmesan cheese shavings
75g roasted peppers in a jar, drained
Balsamic glaze for drizzling
Salt

Serves 2

1] Put the parsley and mint in a small bowl and pour over 100ml of the oil. Add the paprika and walnuts, crushing them roughly with your hands, and season with salt. Stir well and set aside to infuse.

2] Slice the aubergine into rounds, about 1cm thick. Season both sides with salt.

3] Heat the remaining olive oil in a large frying pan over a high heat. Add the aubergine and fry until golden brown and soft. Remove with a slotted spoon and drain on kitchen paper. Meanwhile, cut the mozzarella into rounds about 5mm thick.

4] Place an aubergine slice in the middle of each serving plate and top with some Parmesan shavings, then some roasted pepper and a slice of mozzarella. Drizzle with some of the infused oil. Repeat the process once more and finish with a drizzle of oil and some balsamic glaze. Serve immediately.

ITALIAN-STYLE SMOKED HADDOCK & PAPRIKA OMELETTE

FRITTATINA CON EGLEFINO AFFUMICATO E PAPRICA

Italian-style omelettes, known as frittata or frittatina, are thicker and chunkier than French-style omelettes and are always completely set. All kinds of ingredients are added to the eggs – cheese, vegetables and herbs are the most common – but here I've used smoked haddock and paprika, a great combination. Smoked salmon and black pepper are good too. When making Italian-style omelettes, beat the eggs very lightly (you don't want air bubbles) and cook the omelette slowly. Serve hot with a simply dressed tomato salad.

Serves 2

300ml full-fat milk
3 bay leaves
250g smoked, undyed, skinned haddock fillets
6 medium eggs
1 teaspoon paprika

30g salted butter
2 tablespoons double cream
2 tablespoons chopped fresh chives
Salt

1] Put the milk and 300ml water in a large, shallow pan. Add the bay leaves and bring to the boil. Reduce the heat, add the haddock and simmer gently for about 4 minutes.

2] Transfer the fish to a large plate and leave to cool. Using a fork or your fingers, flake the fish into large chunks. Set aside.

3] Preheat the grill to its highest setting. Break the eggs into a large bowl, add the paprika and season with salt. Whisk and set aside.

4] Melt the butter in a 23cm heavy-based frying pan over a medium heat. Swirl it around to coat the base and sides of the pan. Pour in the eggs and tilt the pan to distribute the eggs evenly over the bottom.

5] When the omelette is set underneath but still very moist on top, sprinkle over the flaked fish and the chives, then drizzle over the cream. Place under the hot grill for about 2 minutes until set firm.

DEEP-FRIED SPICY OYSTERS WITH BALSAMIC DIPPING SAUCE

OSTRICHE FRITTE PICCANTI CON SALSETTA ALL'ACETO BALSAMICO

The ancient Romans loved oysters – they gorged on them at banquets and considered them a great aphrodisiac. British oysters were particularly highly prized and were transported live, packed in barrels of snow, over the Alps to dinner tables in Rome. To satisfy their craving, by the 1st century BCE the Romans had established the world's first oyster farms. Oysters are often eaten raw, but I also like them deep-fried with a piquant dipping sauce, as here.

10 rock oysters
30g plain flour
30g cornflour
1 teaspoon chilli powder
2 tablespoons sesame seeds
150ml chilled bottled soda water

About 1 litre sunflower oil for deep-frying
Salt

For the dipping sauce
3 tablespoons balsamic vinegar
Juice of 1 lemon

Serves 2

1] First remove the oysters from their shells. Place the oyster flat on a tea towel, with the wider end facing you. Wrap your hand in a bundle of tea towels for protection and hold the oyster at the wider end. At the pointed end, insert the tip of a sharp knife (ideally an oyster knife) between the two shells (hold the blade away from you) and prise the shells apart. Remove the oyster and lay on kitchen paper to dry. Repeat for all the oysters, reserving the deeper shells for serving, if desired.

2] To make the dipping sauce, put the vinegar, lemon juice and 3 tablespoons of cold water in a small bowl and whisk to combine. Pour the mixture into a dipping saucer or oyster shell and set aside.

3] To make the batter, put the flour and cornflour in a large bowl with a pinch of salt. Sprinkle over the chilli powder and sesame seeds and mix together. Gradually add the soda water, stirring as you go. The batter should be very thin.

4] Heat the oil in a deep pan or a wok until very hot. To test the temperature, add a small piece of bread; it will sizzle when the oil is hot enough for frying.

5] Dip the oysters in the batter to coat lightly and fry for no more than 1 minute. Drain on kitchen paper. If you like, put the oysters back in their shells. Serve immediately with the dipping sauce alongside.

SALMON ESCALOPES WITH CREAMY VERMOUTH SAUCE

SCALOPPINE DI SALMONE CON SALSA CREMOSA AL VERMOUTH

Light and delicate, these salmon escalopes with a creamy, sweet vermouth sauce are a great option for an elegant supper for two. The fish fillets need to be sliced very thin; to make things simpler, ask your fishmonger to prepare the escalopes for you. Serve with new potatoes and a crispy salad.

Serves 2

400g skinned salmon fillet (middle fillet)
2 tablespoons olive oil

For the sauce
300ml fish stock
100ml double cream

30ml sweet vermouth (e.g. Martini Bianco)
40g salted butter
1 tablespoon freshly squeezed lemon juice
2 tablespoons chopped fresh flat-leaf parsley
White pepper

1] First make the sauce. Heat the stock, half the cream and the vermouth in a medium saucepan over a medium heat. Bring to the boil and let it bubble, stirring occasionally, until the liquid has reduced to about 100ml.

2] Add the remaining cream, butter and lemon juice. Simmer until the sauce has thickened slightly. Stir in the parsley. Set aside.

3] Preheat the grill to its highest setting. Place the salmon, skinned-side down, on a board. Using a long, thin, sharp-bladed knife, cut the fish slightly on the diagonal into 6 slices (escalopes), each about 5mm thick.

4] Line a baking sheet with foil. Lay the escalopes on the sheet and brush both sides with oil. Grill for 30 seconds until just firm and cooked through.

5] Gently warm through the sauce over a low heat. Divide the sauce between 2 serving plates and arrange 3 escalopes per person on top of the sauce. Sprinkle over a little white pepper and serve immediately.

SORRENTO-STYLE LOBSTER WITH LIMONCELLO & ROCKET

ARAGOSTA ALLA SORRENTINA

This is a luxurious dish for a special occasion when you want to impress. Limoncello is a lovely lemon-flavoured liqueur produced in Campania, particularly in the area around Sorrento and Naples (see page 79). It is popular as an *aperitivo* or *digestivo*, but I've used it in this recipe to enhance the dressing, its light, fresh flavour perfectly complementing the richness of the lobster. I have described how to cook live lobsters here, but you can buy cooked lobster from most fishmongers.

Serves 2

2 live lobsters, each about 800g
2 shallots, peeled and very finely sliced
80ml red wine vinegar
5 fresh yellow cherry tomatoes, quartered
5 fresh red cherry tomatoes, quartered
2 tablespoons chopped fresh flat-leaf parsley
Handful of rocket leaves

For the dressing
Juice of ½ lemon
1 tablespoon limoncello liqueur
6 tablespoons extra virgin olive oil
Salt and white pepper

1] Make some air holes in a large plastic bag, place the lobsters in the bag and seal. Transfer immediately to the freezer for 45 minutes.

2] Place the shallots in a small bowl and pour over the vinegar. Leave to marinate for 20 minutes, then drain and set aside.

3] Meanwhile, bring a large pan of water to the boil, add the lobsters and cook for about 8 minutes. Lift out with tongs and set aside to cool.

4] Remove the meat from the lobsters. First twist off the large claws. Using a nutcracker, small hammer or rolling pin, crack the shells of the claws. Pick out the meat and put it in a bowl.

5] Place one lobster body shell on a board, belly-side down. Using a heavy, sharp knife, split the lobster in half lengthways, cutting from the head to the tail. Pull the halves apart. Discard the intestinal tract from the tail and the stomach sac. Remove the meat from the shell and cut into 2cm chunks. Put in the bowl with the claw meat. Retain the shells and remove and discard the legs. Repeat with the second lobster.

6] To make the dressing, put the lemon juice and limoncello in a medium bowl and gradually whisk in the oil. Season with salt and pepper.

7] Transfer the lobster meat to the bowl with the dressing and stir until well coated. Add the tomatoes, drained shallots and parsley and stir to combine. Divide the rocket among the lobster shells and spoon in the lobster mixture.

CHICKEN ESCALOPES WITH WILD MUSHROOMS & THYME

SCALOPPINE DI POLLO CON FUNGHI DI BOSCO E TIMO

Wild mushrooms are extremely popular in Italy, particularly in Calabria – the largest producer of wild mushrooms in Italy – where they grow in the mountainous forests of Sila. The peak season for mushrooms is April to early November, but the season can sometimes extend into late December in the south. Wild mushrooms make a great pairing with chicken and thyme in this classic dish. Serve with a simple tomato salad.

Serves 2

2 skinless, boneless chicken breasts
30g plain flour
1 garlic clove, peeled
6 tablespoons olive oil
1 teaspoon fresh thyme leaves

150g fresh wild mushrooms
4 tablespoons dry white wine
100ml hot chicken stock
1 tablespoon salted butter
Salt and freshly ground black pepper

1] Place the chicken breasts between 2 sheets of cling film. Using a meat mallet or heavy-based saucepan, pound the chicken to make 5mm-thick escalopes. Season both sides with salt and pepper. Coat lightly in the flour and shake off the excess. Set aside. Flatten the garlic with the back of a knife.

2] Heat 3 tablespoons of the oil in a large frying pan over a high heat. Add the garlic and thyme and fry for 30 seconds, stirring continuously. Tip in the mushrooms and fry for 3 minutes. Transfer the mushrooms and garlic to a warm plate and set aside. Wipe the inside of the pan with kitchen paper, ready to be used again.

3] Place the pan over a medium heat and pour in the remaining 3 tablespoons of oil. Add the escalopes and fry for 2 minutes each side. Pour in the wine and cook for 1 minute. When it has evaporated, return the mushrooms and garlic to the pan, add the stock and simmer for 3 minutes. Add the butter and stir for about 30 seconds.

4] To serve, place the escalopes on warmed plates, spoon over the mushrooms (discard the garlic) and pour over the juices from the pan. Serve immediately.

TWICE-BAKED JACKET POTATOES WITH LEEKS & TALEGGIO

PATATE AL FORNO CON PORRI E TALEGGIO

There are few comfort foods that are easier to prepare than baked potatoes, but sometimes they can become a bit repetitive. However, with just a tiny bit more effort you can transform them into something really special for a cosy supper for two. Taleggio is a great melting cheese with a tangy flavour that goes beautifully with the leeks in this recipe. The mascarpone gives a lovely creamy consistency.

Serves 2

2 large baking potatoes
25g salted butter
1 leek, halved lengthways and finely sliced
100g mascarpone cheese

120g Taleggio cheese, rind removed and
 broken into small pieces
Freshly ground black pepper

1] Preheat the oven to 200°C/gas mark 6. Prick the potatoes with a fork several times. Bake for 1½ hours, turning halfway, or until the centre feels soft when you insert a knife into it.

2] Meanwhile, melt the butter in a small pan over a medium heat. Add the leek and fry for 10 minutes or until tender, stirring occasionally. Remove from the heat.

3] Cut the potatoes in half and scoop out the middle, leaving a thin shell. Put the potato flesh and mascarpone into the pan with the leeks. Mash until smooth then stir in the Taleggio.

4] Pile the cheesy potato mixture back into the potato skins and bake for a further 20 minutes. Finish with a few grindings of black pepper. Serve immediately.

SLICED RIB-EYE STEAK WITH BLACK PEPPER BUTTER

TAGLIATA DI MANZO CON BURRO AL PEPE NERO

Tagliata has become increasingly popular in recent years. It is basically a steak that has been cut diagonally into slices and served with the cooking juices and, sometimes, flavoured butter. It is usually placed on a bed of leaves, such as rocket. Here I've given instructions for a medium-rare steak, but if you like it rare, cook it for just 1 minute each side. It's important not to overcook the meat or it will be tasteless and tough. Always remove steaks from the fridge 30 minutes before cooking to bring them to room temperature.

Serves 2

60g salted butter (room temperature)
2 teaspoons coarsely ground black pepper
50g rocket leaves
80g semi-dried tomatoes in oil, drained
2 tablespoons extra virgin olive oil, plus extra
 for brushing

2 rib-eye steaks, about 150g each (room
 temperature)
Sea salt flakes

1] Put the butter in a small bowl with the black pepper and beat together well using a fork or small wooden spoon. Transfer to a sheet of cling film and form into a cylinder by rolling the cling film. Twist the ends to seal and refrigerate for 2 hours. Discard the cling film and slice the butter into 1cm-thick rounds. Return to the fridge.

2] Put the rocket leaves and tomatoes in a bowl, add the oil and toss together. Arrange on a large flat serving platter.

3] Preheat a ridged cast-iron chargrill pan over a high heat for 5–10 minutes or until very hot. Meanwhile, dry the steaks with kitchen paper and brush both sides with oil.

4] Place the steaks in the pan and cook for 2 minutes. Press down with a fish slice but do not move the steaks around while they are cooking. Turn over and place the pepper butter slices on top of the steaks. Sprinkle over a pinch of sea salt flakes. Grill for a further 2 minutes. Remove from the pan and leave to rest for about 2 minutes.

5] To serve, cut the steak diagonally into slices about 1cm thick and arrange on the rocket and tomatoes. Drizzle over any cooking juices from the pan.

Most of Italy's 20 regions have a coastline, so Italians eat a huge amount of fish and shellfish and have a vast selection of wonderful seafood dishes. Even in areas without a coastline, there is plenty of freshwater fish in rivers and lakes, and salt cod (cod that has been preserved in salt and air-dried) is popular throughout the country. Some of the cold dishes in this chapter can be served as a first course, and conversely some of the seafood dishes in the Antipasti & Soups chapter (see pages 11–41) make a good main course — just adjust the portion sizes and add an accompaniment or two.

FISH & SEAFOOD

TUNA TARTARE

SQUID, SPICY SALAMI & BEAN SALAD

SEAFOOD PLATTER WITH TOMATOES & RED CHILLIES

PARMESAN-CRUSTED COD WITH A CREAMY CAPER & PARSLEY SAUCE

CALABRIAN-STYLE KING PRAWNS IN A SPICY TOMATO SAUCE

CAPRI-STYLE PAN-FRIED SEA BREAM

GRILLED TUNA WITH GARLIC GREEN BEANS, TOMATOES & OLIVES

SEA BASS BAKED IN A ROSEMARY-FLAVOURED SALT CRUST

SEA BASS WITH ROASTED VEGETABLES & ANCHOVIES

CREAMY FISH PIE WITH ROASTED RED PEPPERS & VERMOUTH

TUNA TARTARE

TONNO ALLA TARTARA

You'll find variations of this classic dish in restaurants all along the southern Italian coast, especially in Sicily and Calabria. I've tried many different recipes, but this one is my favourite – it's simple, colourful and packed with fresh flavours. When I'm in Italy I drizzle anchovy extract or dripping (*colatura di alici*, see page 79) over the top. This has an amazingly sweet and intense flavour and can be used to enliven plain spaghetti, potatoes, salads and steamed vegetables. You can buy anchovy extract or dripping online and in delicatessens in Britain, but if you can't find it you can drizzle over a little of the olive oil from the anchovy tin.

Serves 4

400g very fresh skinned tuna loin, chopped into 1cm cubes

6 anchovy fillets in oil, drained and roughly chopped

2 tablespoons capers, drained and roughly chopped

3 tablespoons pitted black olives (preferably Leccino), drained and roughly chopped

3 fresh plum tomatoes (preferably San Marzano), deseeded and chopped into 5mm cubes

1 fresh, medium-hot red chilli, deseeded and finely sliced

1 small spring onion, finely chopped

2 tablespoons chopped fresh flat-leaf parsley

2 tablespoons extra virgin olive oil, plus extra for brushing

Grated zest and juice of 1 unwaxed lemon

8 slices of ciabatta

1 garlic clove, peeled

8 leaves of chicory or Little Gem lettuce

2 tablespoons anchovy extract (optional)

1] Put the tuna, anchovies, capers, olives, tomatoes, chilli, spring onion and parsley in a medium bowl. Stir to combine.

2] Pour over the oil and add the lemon zest and juice. Toss everything together gently. Leave for 5 minutes to allow the flavours to combine.

3] Meanwhile, brush both sides of the ciabatta with a little olive oil and toast under the grill until lightly golden. Leave to cool then gently rub the garlic clove over both sides.

4] Place a chicory or lettuce leaf on each plate and pile the tuna mixture into the leaves. Drizzle over the anchovy extract, if using. Serve with the ciabatta.

SQUID, SPICY SALAMI & BEAN SALAD

INSALATA DI CALAMARI CON SALAME PICCANTE E FAGIOLI

I created this dish on the picture postcard Aeolian island of Panarea, where squid is abundant in the surrounding waters. The salad is full of punchy flavours and robust textures and makes a great summer main course.

Serves 4–6

100g tinned chickpeas, rinsed and drained
100g tinned borlotti beans, rinsed and drained
15 fresh red cherry tomatoes, quartered
50g semi-dried cherry tomatoes in oil, drained
125g pitted green olives
1 fresh, medium-hot red chilli, deseeded and finely sliced
1 garlic clove, crushed
3 tablespoons chopped fresh flat-leaf parsley

2 tablespoons freshly squeezed lemon juice
8 tablespoons extra virgin olive oil
400g whole medium squid
80g spicy salami, cut into rounds 5mm thick and halved
50g rocket leaves
Large handful (about 40g) of fresh basil leaves
Salt

1] Put the chickpeas and beans in a large bowl with the fresh and semi-dried tomatoes, olives, chilli, garlic and parsley. Add the lemon juice and 5 tablespoons of the oil, season with salt and toss well to coat. Set aside.

2] To prepare the squid, pull the tentacles from the body. Feel inside the body and remove and discard the 'quill' (a transparent sliver of cartilage). Wash the inside of the body and peel off the outer skin. Cut off the squid tentacles just below the eyes (discard the head and guts). Discard the small, hard beak at the base of the tentacles. Rinse the tentacles and squid body in cold water.

3] Cut open the body pouch of each squid along one side and score the inner side with the tip of a small sharp knife into a fine diamond pattern. Then cut each pouch lengthways in half and then across into 7cm lengths. Keep the tentacles whole.

4] Heat the remaining 3 tablespoons of oil in a large frying pan over a high heat. Add the squid, scored-side up, and the tentacles. Fry for about 1 minute, turning halfway, or until golden and caramelized. Add the salami, season with salt and cook for 1 minute.

5] Add the rocket to the bean mixture, toss until lightly coated in the dressing, and place on a large serving plate. Scatter over the squid and salami, sprinkle over the basil and serve immediately.

SEAFOOD PLATTER WITH TOMATOES & RED CHILLIES

PIATTO DI MARE

All restaurants along the coast in Calabria will offer their own version of this wonderful, spicy mixed seafood platter. It's a great sharing dish for when you're entertaining: it looks stunning and makes a festive and celebratory centrepiece. Either hand the platter around or put it on the table so that everyone can help themselves. Serve with a chilled bottle of Italian white wine and plenty of crusty bread to mop up the delicious sauce.

Serves 6

1kg live clams
1kg live mussels
2 whole medium squid, about 200g in total
4 garlic cloves, peeled and sliced
4 fresh, medium-hot red chillies, deseeded
 and finely sliced
8 tablespoons extra virgin olive oil

6 large whole raw king prawns
150ml dry white wine
300g fresh red cherry tomatoes, halved
4 tablespoons chopped fresh flat-leaf parsley
Salt

1] Soak the clams in cold salted water for 1 hour, drain well and scrub the shells under cold running water. Discard any open clams or clams with broken shells. Set aside.

2] Scrub the mussels under cold running water. Rinse away the grit and remove barnacles with a small, sharp knife. Remove the 'beards' by pulling the dark, stringy pieces away from the mussels. Discard any open mussels or mussels with broken shells. Set aside.

3] To prepare the squid, pull the tentacles from the body. Feel inside the body and remove and discard the 'quill' (a transparent sliver of cartilage). Wash the inside of the body and peel off the outer skin. Cut off the squid tentacles just below the eyes (discard the head and guts). Discard the small, hard beak at the base of the tentacles. Rinse the tentacles and squid body in cold water, place on a board and cut into 2cm pieces. Set aside.

4] Put the garlic and chillies in a large saucepan. Add the oil and place the pan over a medium heat. As soon as the garlic starts to sizzle, add the mussels and clams. Cover and cook for 1 minute or until the mussels and clams just start to open. Tip in the prawns and squid, cover again and cook for 2 minutes.

5] Increase the heat, pour in the wine and cook for 3 minutes, uncovered. Stir in the tomatoes and parsley and season with salt. Cook for a further 3 minutes, stirring occasionally. Discard any mussels and clams that have not opened. Transfer to a large serving platter. Serve immediately.

PARMESAN-CRUSTED COD WITH A CREAMY CAPER & PARSLEY SAUCE

MERLUZZO IN CROSTA DI PARMIGIANO E SALSA AL PREZZEMOLO E CAPPERI

Cod is not native to the Mediterranean (hake is the equivalent), but I know how popular it is in Britain so have adapted this Italian recipe accordingly. The lemon and Parmesan crust adds flavour and contrast in texture and keeps the fish beautifully moist, while the piquant sauce adds pizzazz. It's important to buy sustainable cod: look out for the Marine Stewardship Council (MSC) ecolabel.

80g salted butter (room temperature), cubed
80g fresh white breadcrumbs
80g pine nuts
Grated zest of 1 unwaxed lemon
60g freshly grated Parmesan cheese
Olive oil for greasing
1 whole skinless cod fillet, about 800g
Salt and freshly ground black pepper

For the sauce
500ml fish stock
200ml mascarpone cheese
4 tablespoons capers, drained
3 tablespoons chopped fresh flat-leaf parsley

Serves 4

1] To make the crust, place the butter, breadcrumbs, pine nuts, lemon zest and two-thirds of the Parmesan in a food processor. Season with salt and pepper. Blitz until the mixture binds together. Set aside.

2] Lightly oil a baking sheet. Lay the cod on top, skinned-side down. Season with salt and pepper. Spread the crust mixture in an even layer over the top of the fish. Chill for 30 minutes. Meanwhile, preheat the oven to 200°C/gas mark 6.

3] Sprinkle the remaining Parmesan over the fish and bake for 25 minutes.

4] Meanwhile, make the sauce. Heat the stock in a medium saucepan over a medium heat. Bring to the boil and let it bubble for about 10 minutes or until reduced by two-thirds. Remove the pan from the heat and whisk in the mascarpone. Return the pan to a low heat and simmer for 10 minutes, stirring occasionally. Add the capers and parsley and taste for seasoning.

5] Transfer the cod to a large serving platter and serve with the sauce in a jug.

Parrocchia di Santa Maria Assunta del Lacco - RAVELLO (SA)
Cappella di Santa Maria della Rotonda

...reggiamenti in onore della

Beata Vergine Maria della Rotonda'

6 7 maggio 2017

AZIENDA SANITARIA LOCALE

SALERNO

IL DIRETTORE GENERALE

AVVISA

LA CITTADINANZA CHE IL GIORNO 24 - 05 - 17 AVRÀ

COMUNE DI MINORI   COMUNE DI MINORI

CALABRIAN-STYLE KING PRAWNS IN A SPICY TOMATO SAUCE

GAMBERONI CON NDUJA CALABRESE

Nduja is a spicy salami paste made with hot Calabrian chillies (see pages 26–27). It is so versatile and will seriously transform your cooking – it's hot, sweet and smoky at the same time, and is perfect in sauces or just on its own, spread on thickly sliced bread. Here I paired it with juicy prawns to create the ultimate classy comfort food. You can find nduja online or in Italian delicatessens, but otherwise use 2 teaspoons of dried chilli flakes instead in this recipe – it won't have the same smoky, meaty flavour but will add heat. Serve with toasted ciabatta.

Serves 4

6 tablespoons extra virgin olive oil, plus extra
  for drizzling
6 anchovy fillets in oil, drained
1 medium red onion, peeled and finely sliced
150g pitted black olives (preferably Leccino),
  drained

50g fresh nduja
2 tablespoons capers, drained
3 x 400g tins of chopped tomatoes
100g frozen peas, defrosted
20 large raw king prawns (head and shell on)
4 tablespoons chopped fresh flat-leaf parsley

1] Heat the oil in a large frying pan or wok over a medium heat. Add the anchovies and fry for 3 minutes or until they break down, stirring occasionally. Tip in the onion and fry for about 5 minutes or until slightly softened. Stir in the olives, nduja and capers and fry for about 1 minute.

2] Add the tomatoes and peas and simmer for 6–8 minutes, stirring occasionally.

3] Stir in the prawns and parsley. Cook for about 6 minutes, turning the prawns halfway through cooking.

4] To serve, divide the sauce between 4 bowls or plates and place 5 prawns on top. Drizzle over a little oil. Serve immediately.

CAPRI-STYLE PAN-FRIED SEA BREAM

ORATA ALLA CAPRESE

Simple yet so full of flavour, this is a classic dish from Capri, a beautiful island off the Sorrentine peninsula. Gilthead sea bream is a firm white fish that is extremely popular along Italy's Mediterranean coast. The British equivalent, black bream, has a very short season and is usually available only in late spring, so in Britain you're more likely to find imported gilthead bream. Sea bass, which is similar, and salmon are also good for this recipe.

6 tablespoons extra virgin olive oil
200g fresh red cherry tomatoes, quartered
200g fresh yellow cherry tomatoes, quartered
150g pitted black olives (preferably Leccino),
  drained and halved

About 20 fresh basil leaves, shredded
Juice and grated zest of 1 unwaxed lemon
4 sea bream fillets (about 170g each), skin on
4 tablespoons olive oil
Salt and freshly ground black pepper

Serves 4

1] Heat the extra virgin olive oil in a medium frying pan over a medium heat. Add the tomatoes and olives and fry for 1 minute, stirring occasionally. Stir in the basil and fry for 30 seconds. Add the lemon juice, season with salt and pepper and stir to combine. Set aside.

2] Place the fish fillets on a board and pat dry with kitchen paper. Using a sharp knife, score the fish skin by making 3 diagonal cuts to the point where you can see the flesh. Season with salt and pepper.

3] Heat the olive oil in a large frying pan over a high heat. When the oil is really hot, place the fillets skin-side down in the pan and fry for 3 minutes or until the skin is golden and crisp. (The flesh should be opaque two-thirds of the way up the fillet.) Turn the fillets and fry for 1 further minute.

4] To serve, spoon the tomato and olive mixture onto serving plates and gently place 1 fish fillet on top, with the skin-side uppermost. If you like, sprinkle over a little salt and pepper, add a pinch of lemon zest and serve immediately.

CAMPANIAN SPECIALITIES

Situated on the west coast of southern Italy just above Calabria, Campania has some of the most spectacular scenery in Italy – a dramatic coastline, stunning towns and villages perched high up on the cliffs, and terraces filled with lemon and orange trees sloping down to the sea. Naples, the Amalfi coast, Sorrento, Positano, Ravello, Minori, the island of Capri and the brooding Mount Vesuvius are just some of the highlights of this amazing region. For me, Campania is Italy's larder – you'll find all the ingredients that you associate with Italian cuisine – a great array of pasta, pizzas, buffalo mozzarella and large, ruby-red, gem-like tomatoes – as well as many other local specialities.

AMALFI LEMONS

Huge, succulent, intensely flavoured and gloriously aromatic and sweet, the Amalfi lemon (*sfusato d'Amalfi*, see below) is one of the great prizes of Campania. It grows in abundance on the cliffs above the coast, particularly around Sorrento and Amalfi, and is used in many dishes, both savoury and sweet. Locals sometimes grate its zest over pasta, others eat the flesh on its own. It is also the main ingredient of the drink *limoncello* (see opposite) and is used to make other thirst-quenching drinks, such as *spremuta di limone* (freshly squeezed lemon juice) and *granita* (a semi-frozen dessert or drink). Amalfi lemons are best in summer, as the hot weather makes their flavour even more intense.

SAN MARZANO TOMATOES

The San Marzano plum tomato (see below) – which many chefs consider the best tomato in the world for sauces – thrives in the rich volcanic soil around Mount Vesuvius. It is fleshier than most other tomatoes, with smaller seeds and a robust flavour. These tomatoes are exported all over the world, both fresh and tinned. Officially, they have been named the only tomato that can be used in the 'True Neapolitan pizza' (see opposite).

BUFFALO MOZZARELLA

Water buffalos were introduced to Italy from Asia or the Middle East in the Middle Ages and they were used as draught animals; by the 12th century, their milk was being used to make cheese (although buffalo mozzarella didn't emerge until the 18th century). Produced entirely from buffalo milk, and sometimes referred to as 'white gold' or 'the pearl of the table', *mozzarella di bufala* is a fresh, milky white, stringy-textured cheese that is best eaten the day after it's made. It is a key ingredient in Caprese salad (see page 176) and is also used on pizzas (see page 152). Most imported mozzarella is made from cow's milk and has a firmer, springier consistency and less flavour than buffalo mozzarella.

CACIOCAVALLO CHEESE

Made throughout southern Italy, *caciocavallo* (see opposite) is a hard white aged cheese made from cow's or sheep's milk, with a distinctive gourd-like shape. The name *caciocavallo*, which means 'cheese on horseback', comes from the fact that a pair of cheeses are joined together by a rope and are hung over a wooden beam or board to age. *Caciocavallo* is often served on its own at the end of a meal or is used in cooking.

FISH & SHELLFISH

Seafood is a staple food in Campania, where more people live along the coast than inland. Squid, tuna and anchovies (see below) are very popular, as are clams and mussels. As you would expect, some of the most well-known Campanian dishes have seafood as a main ingredient, including Amalfi-style fish soup (see page 41) and *spaghetti vongole* (see page 132).

PASTA

In the 19th century the Neapolitans were known as 'maccheroni eaters' because of their love of pasta, and today pasta remains extremely popular in the region. Industrial production of dried pasta first started near Naples using durum wheat, and the best-grade pasta is still produced in the town of Gragnano, near Naples. The most popular pasta types are spaghetti, linguine, scialatielli (similar to fettuccine but thicker and shorter), fusilli lunghi (see page 137), ziti (like rigatoni, but a little

thinner and ideal for baking) and paccheri (large tubes that are sometimes stuffed). While in northern Italy the preference is for fresh egg pasta, in the south the pasta is usually dried.

PIZZA

Campania – more specifically Naples – is the home of pizza, and the locals are very proud of their heritage. The Associazione Verace Pizza Napoletana (AVPN) was set up in 1984 to monitor the quality of pizzas and certify chefs in making them the traditional way, using hand-formed dough and designated ingredients for the topping, and baking them in a wood-fired oven for 60–90 seconds. Officially, there are only two types of Neapolitan pizzas that qualify for the trademark 'Vera Pizza Napoletana' – *pizza marinara* (San Marzano tomatoes, extra virgin olive oil, oregano and garlic) and *pizza Margherita* (San Marzano tomatoes, extra virgin olive oil, mozzarella or *fior di latte* cheese, sometimes hard grated cheese, and fresh basil).

COLATURA DI ALICI

A key ingredient in Campanian cooking is *colatura di alici*, or anchovy extract or dripping, which is produced in the small fishing village of Cetara, on the Amalfi coast. Similar to the popular Roman sauce *garum*, it is made by fermenting anchovies in brine, then straining off the juice to use as a flavouring. Anchovy extract is used to add punch to pasta dishes, vegetables, salads and sauces.

LIMONCELLO

Enjoyed as an *aperitivo* before a meal or a *digestivo* at the end, *limoncello* is a sweet lemon liqueur from Campania made from lemon zest from Amalfi lemons, alcohol, water and sugar. It is produced mainly in the area around Naples and Sorrento, on the Amalfi coast and on the islands of Capri, Procida and Ischia. *Limoncello* can be used in cooking, in both savoury dishes (see page 56) and sweet (see page 201).

GRILLED TUNA WITH GARLIC GREEN BEANS, TOMATOES & OLIVES

TONNO GRIGLIATO CON FAGIOLINI VERDI ALL'AGLIO, POMODORI E OLIVE

Chargrilled tuna steak on a bed of green beans, tomatoes and olives makes a tasty, colourful dish for a special summer lunch or a quick supper. It's important not to overcook the tuna: it should be pink in the middle or it will be tough and dry. If you prefer, use green pitted olives or capers in brine instead of black olives. Always buy sustainable tuna from a reputable supplier.

400g fine green beans, trimmed and halved across

4 x 200g tuna steaks (preferably from the loin)

4 tablespoons extra virgin olive oil, plus extra for brushing and drizzling

2 garlic cloves, peeled and sliced

3 large fresh plum tomatoes, deseeded and cut into small cubes

100g pitted black olives (preferably Leccino), drained and halved

4 large fresh mint leaves, shredded

Salt and freshly ground black pepper

Serves 4

1] Bring a small saucepan of salted water to the boil and cook the beans for 3–4 minutes or until al dente. Drain and rinse under cold running water (so they retain their colour and crunch), then drain again thoroughly. Set aside.

2] Preheat a ridged cast-iron chargrill pan over a high heat for 5–10 minutes. Pat the tuna dry with kitchen paper and brush each side with a little oil. Season with salt and pepper. Lay the tuna in the hot pan and cook for 2 minutes each side.

3] Meanwhile, heat the oil over a high heat. Add the drained beans, garlic, tomatoes, olives and mint and fry for 2 minutes, stirring occasionally. Season with salt and pepper.

4] Arrange the vegetables on 4 warm serving plates and place a tuna steak on top (cut in half if the steaks are large). Drizzle over a little oil over and around the tuna and vegetables and grind over some black pepper. Serve immediately.

SEA BASS BAKED IN A ROSEMARY-FLAVOURED SALT CRUST

SPIGOLA IN CROSTA DI SALE AL ROSMARINO

This dish really has the 'wow' factor, so is perfect for entertaining. Imagine your guests' reaction as you bring the tin to the table and crack open the salty crust to reveal the perfectly cooked fish beneath. Baking fish in salt is a very old technique that ensures the fish remains moist. Although you might think the fish would taste incredibly salty, it doesn't, as the salt comes off in large chunks and so is removed before eating. Serve with spinach.

Serves 4

1kg whole sea bass, gutted
3kg rock salt
4 tablespoons chopped fresh rosemary
2 unwaxed lemons, roughly sliced
100g bag crispy mixed salad leaves

For the dressing
100ml extra virgin olive oil
Juice of 1 large lemon
2 tablespoons chopped fresh flat-leaf parsley
Salt and freshly ground black pepper

1] Preheat the oven to 220°C/gas mark 7. Rinse the fish under cold running water and pat dry with kitchen paper.

2] Arrange a layer of salt, 1cm thick, over the bottom of a large roasting tin. Tip the remaining salt into a large bowl and add the rosemary. Mix in enough cold water to moisten the salt slightly, but do not over-wet it; you need to create a stiff slush that can be patted into shape.

3] Place the fish on top of the salt in the tin. Stuff the stomach cavity with the lemons. Cover the top and sides of the fish with the rosemary salt, packing it around the fish to encase it completely. Bake for 25 minutes.

4] Meanwhile, make the dressing. Combine the oil and lemon juice in a small bowl. Slowly pour in 50ml cold water, whisking as you go. Stir in the parsley and season with salt and pepper. Put the salad leaves in a large bowl, pour over a quarter of the dressing and toss to coat. Set aside.

5] To serve, crack open the salt crust with a tablespoon and lift away any large pieces of salt. Use a pastry brush to push away any remaining pieces. Remove the skin with a fork and discard. Run the tip of the fork down the centre of the fish, just to one side of the spine. Gently transfer the fillet to a warm serving plate, then do the same for the second fillet. Turn over the fish and repeat.

6] Drizzle the remaining dressing over the fillets. Serve immediately with the salad on the side.

SEA BASS WITH ROASTED VEGETABLES & ANCHOVIES

SPIGOLA AL FORNO CON VERDURE E ACCIUGHE

Everywhere along the Mediterranean coast in southern Italy you'll find very similar recipes to this using a whole sea bream, salmon, trout and even monkfish. The dish is packed with flavour, and as the vegetables are roasted with the fish, it's a substantial meal in itself and no other accompaniment is needed. If you like a bit of kick, sprinkle over a few pinches of dried chilli flakes.

Serves 4

1 whole sea bass (about 1.6kg), scaled, gutted, gilled, fins and tail trimmed and head removed
100ml extra virgin olive oil, plus extra for brushing
Large pinch of saffron threads
1kg Maris Piper potatoes, peeled and cut into slices 1cm thick

4 large fresh plum tomatoes, quartered lengthways
60g anchovy fillets in oil, drained
150ml hot chicken stock
5 red peppers, deseeded and cut into 8 chunks
6 garlic cloves, halved (skin on)
8 small sprigs of fresh oregano
Salt and freshly ground black pepper

1] Pat the fish dry with kitchen paper and place on a board. Using a sharp knife, score the fish on one side, making 5 diagonal cuts just through to the bones. Score again in the opposite direction to give a criss-cross pattern. Brush all over with oil and season both sides with salt and pepper. Set aside.

2] Preheat the oven to 200°C/gas mark 6. Put the saffron in a small bowl or cup, pour over 3 tablespoons of hot water and set aside to infuse.

3] Bring a large saucepan of salted water to the boil. Add the potatoes, bring back to the boil and simmer for 5 minutes. Drain thoroughly. Arrange the potatoes in a large roasting tin (big enough to hold the sea bass lengthways or diagonally), leaving space around the sides for the red peppers. The potatoes will form a bed for the fish.

4] Scatter the tomatoes and anchovies over the potatoes. Pour over the saffron water (with strands) and the stock. Arrange the peppers around the potatoes and sprinkle over the garlic and oregano. Drizzle the oil over the peppers. Season with salt and pepper. Bake for 15–20 minutes.

5] Remove the tin from the oven and place the fish on top of the potatoes. Bake for about 20 minutes (you know the fish is cooked when the flesh near the bone at the thickest part turns white). Serve immediately.

CREAMY FISH PIE WITH ROASTED RED PEPPERS & VERMOUTH

TORTA DI PESCE CREMOSA CON PEPERONI ARROSTO E VERMOUTH

This is a luxury fish pie with an Italian twist. You can prepare it up to a day ahead, refrigerate it and when you're ready to eat simply pop it in the oven to bake. If making the pie ahead, bring it to room temperature before baking.

Serves 6

Olive oil for greasing
200g skinless salmon fillet, cut into bite-sized chunks
200g skinless cod fillet, cut into bite-sized chunks
200g queen scallops
200g raw king prawns, peeled and deveined
280g roasted red peppers in a jar, drained and sliced

For the topping
750g Desirée potatoes, peeled and cut into large chunks
80g salted butter (room temperature), cut into small cubes

2 large egg yolks
80g freshly grated Grana Padano cheese
Salt and freshly ground black pepper

For the sauce
3 tablespoons olive oil
50g salted butter
1 large red onion, peeled and finely chopped
1 tablespoon fresh thyme leaves
100ml sweet vermouth (e.g. Martini bianco)
4 tablespoons plain flour
250ml hot fish stock
200ml full-fat milk
5 tablespoons double cream
3 tablespoons chopped fresh flat-leaf parsley

1] To make the topping, cook the potatoes in simmering salted water for 15–20 minutes or until tender. Drain then pass through a potato ricer or mash until smooth. Add the butter and leave to cool slightly. Stir in the egg yolks and season with salt and pepper. Set aside. Preheat the oven to 190°C/gas mark 5.

2] To make the sauce, heat the oil and butter in a medium saucepan over a medium heat. Add the onion and thyme and fry for 5–10 minutes, stirring occasionally. Pour in the vermouth and simmer for about 3 minutes. Stir in the flour and cook for 1–2 minutes.

3] Gradually add the stock, stirring constantly, until smooth. Simmer for 5 minutes or until reduced by one-third. Stir in the milk, reduce the heat and simmer for 3 minutes or until the sauce thickens. Stir in the cream and parsley and season with salt and pepper. Set aside.

4] Grease a 2-litre pie dish with oil and place on a baking sheet. Put the fish, scallops, prawns and peppers in the dish. Season with salt and pepper. Pour the sauce over the seafood mixture and stir to combine. Leave to cool.

5] Spread the topping evenly over the surface. Sprinkle over the Grana Padano. Bake for 30 minutes until golden. Leave to stand for 5 minutes before serving.

Although seafood is very prevalent along the coast in Italy, meat is still extremely popular wherever you go. Pork is probably the most widely available meat, both fresh and cured, as well as chicken — a particular favourite in Tuscany. Beef and veal are most popular in the north, where much of the land is pasture, and lamb is eaten mainly in the mountainous central and southern regions. Many other types of meat that are not at all popular in Britain are enjoyed in Italy, including kid and rabbit, and I have provided recipes for both in this chapter. They taste incredible, and I believe it's important to keep on experiencing new things in life — and that includes new foods. So please do try them — you will be really glad that you did!

MEAT & POULTRY

HERB & MUSTARD-CRUSTED RACK OF LAMB

STUFFED PORK ROLLS IN A TOMATO SAUCE

MAMMA ALBA'S MEATBALLS

POT-ROASTED BEEF IN RED WINE

RED WINE & CHERRY GRAVY

BEEF FILLET WITH PARMA HAM & PESTO IN PUFF PASTRY

ROAST BEEF WITH ROASTED VEGETABLES & FRESH HERBS

TUSCAN-STYLE BARBECUED PORK WITH SPICY BEANS

ROASTED KID WITH GARLIC NEW POTATOES

SWEET & SOUR RABBIT WITH BORETTANE ONIONS

CRISPY CHICKEN WITH A SPICY SAUCE & GREEN BEANS

SPICY CHICKEN WITH NEW POTATOES, TOMATOES & RED PEPPERS

ITALIAN-STYLE ROAST CHICKEN WITH NEW POTATOES & RED ONION

CHARGRILLED CHICKEN WITH GARLIC & ROSEMARY POTATOES

HERB & MUSTARD-CRUSTED RACK OF LAMB

COSTOLETTE D'AGNELLO IN CROSTA DI SENAPE ED ERBE

Lamb is eaten mainly in central and southern Italy, although roasted young spring lamb is traditional throughout the country at Easter. Later in the year, a rack of lamb makes a wonderful dish for a special occasion. Cooking the lamb on the bone and coating it in a herb crust keeps the meat really moist and succulent. Serve with roasted baby new potatoes and green beans.

Serves 4

2 racks of lamb (about 350g each), trimmed
   of excess fat
25g fresh white breadcrumbs
2 tablespoons chopped fresh flat-leaf parsley
1 tablespoon chopped fresh rosemary

1 tablespoon chopped fresh mint
15g freshly grated Parmesan cheese
2 tablespoons olive oil
2 tablespoons English mustard
Salt and freshly ground black pepper

1] Preheat the oven to 200°C/gas mark 6. Season the lamb with salt and pepper.

2] Place the breadcrumbs, parsley, rosemary and mint in a food processor and blitz. Tip into a small bowl and stir in the Parmesan. Set aside.

3] Heat the oil in a large non-stick frying pan over a high heat. When very hot, sear the lamb for about 2 minutes each side or until browned.

4] Transfer the lamb to a baking sheet, flesh-side up. Spread over the mustard. Press the herb crumbs into the mustard.

5] Roast for 15–20 minutes. Remove from the oven, cover with foil and leave to rest in a warm place for 5 minutes before serving. To serve, slice into cutlets.

STUFFED PORK ROLLS IN A TOMATO SAUCE

INVOLTINI DI MAIALE IN SALSA DI POMODORO

There are many variations on the theme of stuffed pork rolls in southern Italy – they may be filled with cheese, prosciutto, sultanas, pine nuts and a variety of other ingredients. In this recipe, thin slices of pork are stuffed with minced pork back fat, parsley and garlic, then browned and simmered in a tomato sauce. Your butcher may be able to supply pork back fat if they make their own sausages, but if you can't find it use unsmoked bacon instead.

Serves 6

125g pork back fat, minced
3 tablespoons chopped fresh flat-leaf parsley
4 garlic cloves, peeled (2 crushed, 2 left whole)
6 pork shoulder steaks, trimmed

3 tablespoons olive oil
2 x 400g tins of chopped tomatoes
6 fresh basil leaves, shredded
Salt and freshly ground black pepper

1] Place the pork back fat, parsley and crushed garlic in a small bowl. Season with salt and pepper. Mix until smooth. Set aside.

2] Place each pork steak between 2 sheets of cling film. Using a meat mallet or heavy-based pan, pound the steak to about 5mm thick. Season with salt.

3] Spread the pork back fat mixture evenly over one side of the pork slices. Roll up and tie with kitchen string to secure.

4] Heat the oil in a flameproof casserole over a medium heat. Add the pork rolls in batches and fry for 8 minutes, turning a couple of times until lightly browned on all sides. Using a slotted spoon, transfer the rolls to a plate.

5] Put the 2 whole garlic cloves in the casserole and fry for 1 minute. Add the tomatoes and basil and season with salt. Bring to the boil then return the pork rolls to the casserole together with any meat juices. Gently submerge the rolls in the sauce. Reduce the heat and simmer for 1 hour, uncovered.

6] To serve, divide the sauce among 6 serving plates (discard the garlic), remove the string from the rolls and arrange the rolls on the sauce. If you like, grind over a little black pepper.

MAMMA ALBA'S MEATBALLS

POLPETTE DI MAMMA ALBA

The secret of my mother's meatballs is very simple – always use two types of mincemeat for texture and flavour (in this case pork and beef) and keep the tomato sauce simple, so you can appreciate the flavour of the meatballs. She also used to bake the meatballs before simmering them in the tomato sauce rather than frying them, as is often the case. Always use fresh breadcrumbs rather than dried or toasted, or the meatballs will be tough and chewy. Serve with plenty of warm crusty bread to mop up the sauce.

Olive oil for greasing
400g minced pork
400g minced beef
150g fresh white breadcrumbs
2 garlic cloves, peeled and crushed
5 tablespoons chopped fresh flat-leaf parsley
100g freshly grated Grana Padano cheese
2 medium eggs, lightly beaten
Salt and freshly ground black pepper

For the sauce
2 x 400g tins of chopped tomatoes
690ml jar of passata (sieved tomatoes)
4 tablespoons extra virgin olive oil
½ teaspoon dried chilli flakes
10 fresh basil leaves, plus extra to garnish

Serves 4

1] Preheat the oven to 220°C/gas mark 7. Grease a large baking sheet with oil and set aside. Place the pork, beef, breadcrumbs, garlic, parsley, Grana Padano and eggs in a large bowl. Season with salt and pepper. Mix with your hands until everything is thoroughly combined.

2] Using dampened hands, take small amounts of the meat mixture and roll into 12 equal-sized balls. Place the balls on the baking sheet. Bake for 12 minutes.

3] Meanwhile, make the sauce. Put the tomatoes, passata and oil in a large saucepan over a medium heat. Stir in the chilli flakes, basil and some salt. Bring to the boil. Reduce the heat, partially cover the pan and simmer for 10 minutes, stirring occasionally.

4] Carefully place the meatballs in the tomato sauce and partially cover the pan again. Simmer for 30 minutes, turning the meatballs occasionally. If the sauce gets too thick, add a little hot water. To serve, scatter over a few basil leaves.

POT-ROASTED BEEF IN RED WINE

STUFATO DI MANZO AL VINO ROSSO

Beef is generally more common in northern Italy than in the central and southern parts of the country, but it is the most popular meat in the Lazio region, particularly in Rome. When bought in a single piece it is often braised for a long time in red wine, with onions, carrots, celery and fresh herbs, as in this recipe. The long, slow cooking time allows the meat to cook to a melting softness. Serve with creamy mashed potato.

Serves 4

1kg beef topside, trimmed
4 tablespoons olive oil
2 large red onions, peeled and finely sliced
2 large carrots, peeled and sliced into 5mm
  rounds
2 celery sticks, cut into 5mm slices
300ml hot beef stock

300ml full-bodied red wine
2 tablespoons tomato purée
2 bay leaves
2 sprigs of fresh rosemary
3 sprigs of fresh thyme
Salt and freshly ground black pepper

1] Preheat the oven to 160°C/gas mark 3. Season the beef well all over with salt and pepper.

2] Heat 2 tablespoons of the oil in a large flameproof casserole over a medium heat. Add the onions, carrots and celery and fry for 10 minutes, stirring occasionally. Using a slotted spoon, transfer the vegetables to a large plate and set aside.

3] Heat the remaining 2 tablespoons of oil in the casserole. When the oil is very hot, sear the beef all over for about 3 minutes or until browned. Remove the beef and set aside.

4] Pour in the stock, scraping up all the sticky bits from the bottom of the pan. Add the wine and bring to the boil. Reduce the heat and simmer for 1 minute. Stir in the tomato purée and herbs. Season with salt and pepper.

5] Return the vegetables and meat to the casserole, bring to simmering point and cover. Cook in the oven for 1 hour and 20 minutes, turning the meat and stirring the vegetables after about 50 minutes. Discard the herbs.

6] To serve, slice the beef and arrange it on a large serving platter. Spoon over the vegetables and the sauce.

RED WINE & CHERRY GRAVY

SALSINA AL VINO ROSSO ED AMARENE

This delicious gravy goes beautifully with a variety of beef dishes, including my Beef fillet with Parma ham and pesto in puff pastry (see page 102) and Roast beef with roasted vegetables and fresh herbs (see page 106). I make it using amarena cherries, which grow in the upper plains of Sorrento. They are quite bitter so are usually preserved in syrup. If you can't find amarena cherries, use red cherries in syrup or 2 tablespoons of cherry jam instead.

3 tablespoons olive oil

1 large red onion, peeled and finely sliced

1 teaspoon salt

3 sprigs of fresh rosemary

1 tablespoon runny honey

500ml full-bodied red wine

400ml hot chicken stock

2 tablespoons balsamic vinegar

1½ teaspoons cornflour

200g pitted cherries in syrup

Serves 4

1] Heat the oil in a medium saucepan over a medium heat. Add the onion and salt and fry for 8 minutes, stirring occasionally. Add the rosemary and honey and fry for 1 minute. Pour in the wine and bring to the boil. Reduce the heat to low and simmer gently for 15 minutes, stirring occasionally.

2] Add the stock and vinegar and simmer for 20 minutes, stirring occasionally. Meanwhile, put the cornflour in a small cup or bowl and stir in 3 tablespoons of water. Set aside.

3] Place a sieve over a medium bowl and pour in the gravy. Using the back of a wooden spoon, press the gravy through. Return the sieved gravy to the saucepan and place over a low heat.

4] Stir in the cornflour mixture, whisking constantly for 1 minute to remove any lumps. When it has thickened slightly, add the cherries and stir for 1 minute.

BEEF FILLET WITH PARMA HAM & PESTO IN PUFF PASTRY

FILETTO DI MANZO IN CAMICIA

This is a classic dish that I learnt at catering college in Naples. It is very similar to beef Wellington – fillet steak wrapped in puff pastry and baked – but uses Italian ingredients such as Parma ham and red pesto instead of pâté and mushrooms. For best results, the beef should be medium rare in the middle. Serve with my delicious Red wine and cherry gravy (see page 101).

Serves 4

800g piece of middle-cut beef fillet, trimmed
5 tablespoons olive oil
10 slices of Parma ham
4 tablespoons shop-bought red, sun-dried
  tomato pesto

500g puff pastry
4 egg yolks
Salt and freshly ground black pepper

1] Wrap a tight layer of cling film around the beef to form a cylinder, then wrap it around twice more for reinforcement. Chill overnight.

2] Heat the oil in a large frying pan over a high heat. Remove the cling film from the beef and season with salt and pepper. When the oil is very hot, sear the meat for 1 minute on all sides – it should be brown all over but still rare in the middle. Remove from the pan and leave to cool.

3] Arrange the Parma ham on a large sheet of cling film, overlapping the slices slightly. Spread a layer of red pesto over the ham. Place the beef in the centre of the ham. Using the cling film, wrap the ham around the beef to create a neat, tight log. Twist the ends of the cling film to seal. Chill for 45 minutes.

4] Roll out the pastry on a lightly floured surface to a rectangle large enough to envelop the beef with a little overlap and allowing about 20cm (8in) extra at either end. Remove the cling film and place the beef in the middle of the pastry. Wrap the pastry tightly around the beef to enclose. Press the edges firmly to seal. Wrap tightly with cling film and chill for 1 hour. Meanwhile, preheat the oven to 200°C/gas mark 6.

5] Remove the cling film. Using the back of a knife, lightly score a line down the centre, then diagonal lines either side to create a herringbone pattern. Beat the egg yolks and add 2 tablespoons of water and a pinch of salt. Brush the outside of the pastry case with the egg and season generously with salt and pepper.

6] Bake for 30 minutes for medium rare, or 10 minutes longer for medium. If the pastry browns too quickly, cover with foil. Remove from the oven and leave to rest for 10 minutes. Cut into thick slices to serve – use a serrated knife to slice through the pastry and ham, then finish with a sharp carving knife for the meat.

ROAST BEEF WITH ROASTED VEGETABLES & FRESH HERBS

ARROSTO DI MANZO CON VERDURE ED ERBE FRESCHE

Historically, Italy is associated more with pork than beef, as pigs are less expensive to raise and easier to butcher than cows. However, the post-war boom brought new wealth to Italy and for the first time in the country's history the average Italian began sitting down to beef for dinner. This dish is one of many cooked by the beautiful people from Catanzaro Lido in the Calabria region. Serve with crispy roast potatoes and Red wine and cherry gravy (see page 101).

Serves 4

2 leeks, roughly chopped
2 medium carrots, peeled and roughly chopped
2 celery sticks, roughly chopped
1 large fennel bulb, cored and quartered
10 garlic cloves (skin on), halved
8 sprigs of fresh thyme

2 sprigs of fresh rosemary
6 sprigs of fresh sage
4 tablespoons extra virgin olive oil
1.5kg beef topside
Salt and freshly ground black pepper

1] Preheat the oven to 240°C/gas mark 9. Put all the vegetables (including the garlic) and herbs in a large roasting tin, about 25 x 30cm. Drizzle over 2 tablespoons of the oil and season with salt and pepper. Using your hands, mix thoroughly so the vegetables are coated in the oil. Spread out the vegetables over the bottom of the tin.

2] Season the beef with salt and pepper and place it on the vegetables. Drizzle over the remaining 2 tablespoons of oil.

3] Reduce the oven temperature to 200°C/gas mark 6 and roast for 1 hour (for medium rare), basting halfway through. Increase the cooking time by 10 minutes if you prefer your beef well done and reduce by 10 minutes if you like it rare.

4] Transfer the beef to a carving board, cover loosely with foil and leave to rest for 10–15 minutes. Meanwhile, transfer the vegetables to a serving dish and keep warm. To serve, cut the meat into slices and serve with the vegetables.

TUSCAN-STYLE BARBECUED PORK WITH SPICY BEANS

MAIALE GRIGLIATO ALLA TOSCANA CON FAGIOLI PICCANTI

After an afternoon of herding cattle with the Tuscan *butteri* (cowboys), I knew the best way to end the day was to have a hearty barbecue on the beach. You just can't beat a pile of sticky ribs, plump sausages, pork chops and steaks and marinated grilled vegetables, washed down with a few beers or a stiff whisky. If you prefer, the meat can be cooked in the oven at 180°C/gas mark 4 (15–30 minutes depending on the meat) and the beans on the hob (about 15 minutes).

Serves 6

4 pork ribs
4 pork loin steaks
6 pork sausages
4 pork chops
2 fennel bulbs, cored and cut into 3 thick
 pieces
6 cobs sweetcorn
2 large red peppers, deseeded and quartered
4 Romano (long, thin) peppers (left whole)

For the marinade
4 tablespoons olive oil
4 tablespoons balsamic vinegar
50ml red wine
2 tablespoons runny honey

3 tablespoons whisky
3 teaspoons chilli powder
2 teaspoons paprika
2 teaspoons fine sea salt

For the beans
2 tablespoons olive oil
2 medium red onions, finely sliced
3 x 400g tins of borlotti beans, rinsed and
 drained
3 teaspoons chilli powder
3 teaspoons paprika
100ml red wine
Small handful of fresh oregano, shredded

1] Put the meat on a large platter or tray. Add the ingredients for the marinade and mix together with your hands until well coated. Ideally, marinate for 4–5 hours (or minimum 30 minutes).

2] Light the barbecue. When the barbecue is ready (the coals will be covered in a fine greyish white ash), make the beans. Heat the oil in a heavy-based saucepan at the edge of the grill (where the temperature is lower). When hot add the onions and fry for about 5 minutes or until soft, stirring frequently. Add the beans, chilli powder and paprika and stir to combine. Pour in the wine and a dash of water and add the oregano. Cook for 20–25 minutes, stirring occasionally.

3] Take the meat out of the marinade (reserve the marinade). Place the ribs on the barbecue and grill for 8–10 minutes, then add the loin steaks and sausages and cook for 7–8 minutes, then the chops and cook for 5–6 minutes. Turn occasionally but do not move the meat around too much. Meanwhile, lightly coat the vegetables in the leftover marinade. Place the fennel and corn on the barbecue and cook for 8–10 minutes then the peppers and cook for 5 minutes.

LAZIO SPECIALITIES

Located in central Italy, between Tuscany in the north and Campania in the south, Lazio lies at the heart of the country. Its capital is Rome, so the region has a longstanding gastronomic tradition of fine food that dates back over two thousand years, as well as simpler, more rustic fare. Beef and veal are the meat of choice, with *saltimbocca* and braised oxtail being two well-known dishes from the region, but pork, chicken, kid, lamb, rabbit and offal are also popular. The fertile volcanic soil is ideal for cultivating vegetables and fruit, including grapes for wine-making.

OLIVES

Southern Lazio is famous for its wonderful black Gaeta olives. Similar to the Greek Kalamata olives, they have a meaty texture and are considered the best olives for cooking (see page 115), but they are also eaten on their own, in salads or chopped and made into a tapenade.

ONANO LENTILS

Known as the 'lentil of the popes', Onano lentils have been cultivated in the sandy volcanic soils around Onano, in the province of Viterbo, north of Rome, for centuries. They are light brown, with grey, pink or green marbling, and have an intense flavour and creamy consistency. In many regions of Italy, lentils are eaten on New Year's Eve or New Year's Day, as they are believed to bring wealth for the forthcoming year, their round shape being reminiscent of small coins.

ARTICHOKES

The best artichokes in Italy are found in the rich soil of Lazio, in the area around Rome. There are many different varieties, including very small ones that are eaten raw or preserved in oil and served as part of a mixed antipasti. The most famous Lazio dishes using artichokes are *carciofi alla giudea*, from Rome's Jewish quarter, in which artichokes are deep-fried whole in olive oil, and *carciofi alla romana*, in which larger artichokes are stuffed with herbs, breadcrumbs and garlic and baked. The famous festival *Sagra del carciofo romanesco*, which takes place each year in April, celebrates this much-loved vegetable.

BACCALÀ

Traditionally eaten on Fridays, which were decreed 'meatless' days by the Roman Catholic Church, *baccalà* (salt cod) is a staple food in Lazio. It is basically cod that has been preserved by salting then drying. Each region of Italy has its own specialities, but in Lazio it is *baccalà alla romana*, which is salt cod coated in a light batter and deep-fried. It is also often cooked in a tomato sauce with onions and white wine (*baccalà in guazzetto*) or eaten cold in a salad with potatoes (see page 13).

FISH & SHELLFISH

Along the Lazio coast seafood is popular, particularly red mullet, octopus and crustaceans. A great delicacy of the region is the delicately flavoured *mazzancolla*, or *gambero imperiale* (see below), which is a kind of giant king prawn harvested in summer and traditionally served fried or grilled. There is also a lot of freshwater fish from rivers and lakes, including eels.

GUANCIALE

Many meats are cured in Lazio, including *guanciale*. Resembling *pancetta*, *guanciale* is pork cheek that has been salted, rolled in pepper and dried. The curing process lasts about three months. It is often used in cooking, and is the main ingredient in Lazio's pasta speciality *spaghetti all'amatriciana*. Good-quality *guanciale* can also be eaten raw.

CHEESE

Lazio has a strong cheese-making tradition, with the sheep's milk cheese *pecorino romano*, buffalo mozzarella (*mozzarella di bufala*) and *ricotta romana* (see below) being the most popular cheeses in the region. *Ricotta romana* is made from sheep's milk and is eaten either fresh, within days of being made, or it is salted and preserved. It is also used in cooking, for example in tarts, pastries and fritters. *Provatura* (a buffalo milk cheese similar to *mozzarella*) is also popular in Lazio.

PASTA

Some of the most well-known pasta sauces originate in Lazio, including *carbonara* (eggs and *pancetta* or *guanciale*), *amatriciana* (*guanciale*, tomatoes, onions and chilli), *puttanesca* (anchovies, chillies and tomatoes) and *arrabbiata* (a very spicy tomato sauce with chilli). The pasta itself is usually long, such as spaghetti, or tube-shaped, to absorb the hearty sauces.

GNOCCHI

Potato gnocchi are very popular in Lazio, where they're usually made from yellow waxy potatoes and egg (in some regions of Italy they're made from starchy potatoes and no egg). Frequently, they're dressed with the local's favourite – *amatriciana* sauce. Another speciality of Lazio is *gnocchi alla romana*, also known as *gnocchi di semolino*, as they're made from semolina instead of potatoes. This type of gnocchi tend to be served with a creamy sauce, such as béchamel, or simply cream and Parmesan.

TIELLA

A speciality of Gaeta, in southern Lazio, *tiella* (see below) is an enclosed pie made from pizza dough and filled with vegetables and sometimes seafood. Popular as a street food, it is named for the round baking dish in which it is cooked (*tiella* in southern Italy, *teglia* in standard Italian); traditionally this was earthenware but today it is usually metal. When I was filming in Gaeta recently I made *tiella* from escarole (a slightly bitter-tasting, leafy green vegetable in the chicory family) and chillies. It's simple food, but oh-so moreish!

ROASTED KID WITH GARLIC NEW POTATOES

CAPRETTO AL FORNO E PATATE NOVELLE ALL'AGLIO

Kid (young goat) is eaten mainly in central and southern Italy, particularly in mountainous regions. It has a delicate flavour and is similar to lamb, but kid is slightly sweeter, leaner and firmer. It hasn't yet taken off in Britain, which is a pity, as it's delicious and relatively healthy too, having fewer calories than beef, pork, lamb and even chicken. It isn't available in supermarkets, but you may find it at a good local butcher's or farmer's market, and there are specialist suppliers online. Kid meat benefits from long, slow cooking and can become tough if cooked at high temperatures or with insufficient liquid. Don't treat it like lamb and serve it rare; it should be cooked thoroughly, or it will be tough.

Serves 6

3kg kid (bone-in), trimmed and cut into
  18 pieces
5 garlic cloves, peeled and crushed
2 tablespoons chopped fresh rosemary
100ml extra virgin olive oil
4 tablespoons runny honey
100ml hot lamb stock
300ml dry white wine
Salt and freshly ground black pepper

For the potatoes
1kg baby new potatoes (preferably Charlotte),
  scrubbed and quartered lengthways into fat
  chips
6 garlic cloves, peeled and crushed
2 tablespoons chopped fresh rosemary
140ml extra virgin olive oil

1] Preheat the oven to 200°C/gas mark 6. Season the meat with salt and pepper and place in a large roasting tin, about 45 x 35cm, in a single layer.

2] Add the garlic and rosemary. Drizzle over the olive oil and honey and, using your hands, mix together thoroughly to coat the meat. Cover the tin with foil.

3] Roast for 1 hour. Remove the tin from the oven and discard the foil. Turn the meat. Pour in the stock and wine. Return to the oven for a further 45 minutes, turning the meat halfway.

4] Meanwhile, divide the potatoes and garlic between 2 smaller roasting tins, about 25 x 30cm each. Sprinkle over the rosemary and drizzle with the olive oil. Using your hands, toss the potatoes and garlic thoroughly until well coated in the oil. Season with salt and pepper. Roast for 1 hour, turning several times.

5] Remove the meat and potatoes from the oven. Tip the potatoes into the roasting tin with the meat and toss gently in the juices. Serve immediately.

SWEET & SOUR RABBIT WITH BORETTANE ONIONS

CONIGLIO IN AGRODOLCE CON CIPOLLE BORETTANE

Many families in Italy make use of the abundant ingredients on their doorstep – fish caught from the sea, and rabbit, vegetables and herbs from their own back gardens. This recipe came from a wonderful farming family who live near Torre del Greco in Campania – the town where I was born. If you don't fancy eating rabbit, use chicken thighs and legs instead, and if you can't get hold of Borettane onions, small pickled onions in balsamic vinegar make a good substitute.

Serves 4

50g plain flour
1 large rabbit (about 1.8kg), including the liver, heart and kidneys, cut into 8 pieces
6 tablespoons olive oil
1 large red onion, peeled and thinly sliced
75g shallots, peeled and sliced
1 celery stick, cut into 1cm cubes
1 large carrot, peeled and cut into 1cm dice
25g sun-dried tomatoes, drained and finely chopped
1 teaspoon fennel seeds
350ml red wine vinegar

50g brown sugar
2 tablespoons tomato purée
1 litre hot chicken stock
100g Borettane onions in balsamic vinegar, drained
75g pitted black olives (preferably Leccino), drained
40g sultanas
1 tablespoon fresh thyme leaves
25g toasted pine nuts
Salt and freshly ground black pepper

1] Preheat the oven to 180°C/gas mark 4. Put the flour on a large plate and season with salt and pepper. Dust the rabbit pieces with the seasoned flour.

2] Heat 4 tablespoons of the oil in a large flameproof casserole over a medium to high heat. When very hot, add half the rabbit and fry for about 5 minutes each side or until golden brown all over. Transfer to a large plate using a slotted spoon and set aside. Repeat for the remaining rabbit.

3] Add the red onion, shallots, celery, carrot, sun-dried tomatoes and fennel seeds. Fry for about 5 minutes, stirring occasionally. Stir in the vinegar, sugar and tomato purée. Cook for 5 minutes, stirring occasionally. Return the rabbit and any juices to the casserole. Add the stock and bring to the boil. Transfer to the oven, uncovered, for 20 minutes.

4] Remove from the oven and add the Borettane onions, olives, sultanas and thyme. Season with salt and pepper. Return to the oven for a further 25 minutes or until the rabbit is cooked through.

5] Heat the remaining 2 tablespoons of oil in a small frying pan. Add the offal and fry for 2 minutes, turning halfway. Season with salt and pepper. To serve, put the rabbit and offal on a serving platter and pour over the juices. Garnish with pine nuts.

[113]

CRISPY CHICKEN WITH A SPICY SAUCE & GREEN BEANS

COTOLETTA DI POLLO CON SALSA PICCANTE E FAGIOLINI VERDI

My aunty Clara is the eldest of my mother's nine sisters and has always been like a second mother to me. When I was a little boy I used to spend every Thursday and Friday afternoon with her and she would often cook this wonderful dish for me. I just love the contrast of textures and flavours – the crispy, Parmesan-coated chicken with the spicy tomato and olive sauce.

3 tablespoons plain flour
3 medium eggs
80g freshly grated Parmesan cheese
60g dried breadcrumbs
4 skinless, boneless chicken breasts
4 tablespoons olive oil
40g Parmesan cheese shavings

For the sauce
3 tablespoons olive oil
2 garlic cloves, peeled and sliced

1 teaspoon dried chilli flakes
2 x 400g tins of chopped tomatoes
150g pitted black olives (preferably Gaeta or
  Leccino), drained
Salt

For the beans
400g fine green beans
50ml extra virgin olive oil
2 tablespoons white wine vinegar

Serves 4

1] First prepare the sauce. Heat the oil in a medium saucepan over a medium heat. Add the garlic. As soon as it starts to sizzle, add the chilli flakes and fry for 1 minute, stirring continually. Tip in the tomatoes and olives and bring to the boil. Reduce the heat and simmer for 20 minutes, uncovered, stirring occasionally. Season with salt. Set aside.

2] Put the flour on a large plate or tray. Beat the eggs in a large bowl and season with salt. Combine the grated Parmesan and breadcrumbs in a shallow dish. Place the chicken breasts between 2 sheets of cling film. Using a rolling pin, meat mallet or heavy-based pan, pound the chicken to about 1cm thick. Dip each chicken breast in the flour, then the eggs, then finally the breadcrumb mixture. Ensure each breast is evenly coated and press the breadcrumbs firmly into the egg so they stick.

3] Heat the oil in a large frying pan over a medium heat. Add the chicken and fry for 4–5 minutes each side. Drain on kitchen paper. Keep warm.

4] Meanwhile, plunge the beans into boiling water for 2–3 minutes or until al dente. Using a slotted spoon, transfer to a large bowl. While still warm, drizzle over the oil and vinegar, season well and toss to coat.

5] Gently warm through the sauce over a low heat. Divide the sauce among 4 serving plates, then place the chicken breast on the sauce. Scatter over the Parmesan shavings. Serve the beans on the side.

SPICY CHICKEN WITH NEW POTATOES, TOMATOES & RED PEPPERS

POLLO PICCANTE CON PATATE NOVELLE, POMODORI E PEPERONI ROSSI

This is an incredibly simple recipe, perfect for a midweek supper – you just put everything in the roasting tin and pop it in the oven. Being a one-pot dish, minimal washing-up is required and there's no need to cook any additional vegetables, although you may like to serve it with a mixed salad. Make sure you use a large enough roasting tin – ideally the ingredients should be in a single layer so the chicken will turn golden brown, the peppers and onion will start to char around the edges and the potatoes will become lovely and crisp all over.

650g baby new potatoes (preferably Charlotte), scrubbed and halved lengthways

6 fresh plum tomatoes, quartered

1 large red onion, peeled, halved and cut into 1cm slices

2 red peppers, deseeded and cut into 2cm chunks

1 tablespoon dried oregano

1kg chicken legs (skin on)

1kg bone-in chicken thighs (skin on)

75ml olive oil

1 teaspoon chilli powder

Salt

Serves 6

1] Preheat the oven to 220°C/gas mark 7. Put the potatoes, tomatoes, onion and red peppers in a large roasting tin, about 45 x 35cm. Sprinkle over the oregano and season with salt.

2] Season the chicken with salt, put it in the tin and drizzle over the oil. Using your hands, mix thoroughly until the vegetables and chicken are well coated in oil. Arrange the chicken on top of the vegetables, skin-side up. Sprinkle over the chilli powder.

3] Roast for 45 minutes. Remove from the oven and turn over the chicken. Return to the oven for 35 minutes.

ITALIAN-STYLE ROAST CHICKEN WITH NEW POTATOES & RED ONION

POLLO ARROSTO CON PATATE NOVELLE E CIPOLLE ROSSE

Italians love the combination of chicken, lemon and fresh herbs. In this recipe I've put a mixture of olive oil, Italian herbs and lemon zest under the skin of the chicken, as it imparts such a lovely delicate flavour and also helps to keep the meat moist. New potatoes and red onion go beautifully with the chicken. You can either use whole baby new potatoes or cut them into chunks, as I've done here. I've used thyme in the potatoes, but feel free to play about with the herbs.

3 tablespoons extra virgin olive oil
Grated zest and juice of 1 unwaxed lemon
1 tablespoon chopped fresh oregano
1 tablespoon chopped fresh rosemary
1 tablespoon shredded fresh basil
1 whole free-range chicken, about 2kg
2 bay leaves
Salt and freshly ground black pepper

For the potatoes
1kg new potatoes, scrubbed and cut into
 large chunks
1 large red onion, peeled, quartered and cut
 into slices 1cm thick
1 tablespoon fresh thyme leaves
2 tablespoons extra virgin olive oil

Serves 6

1] Preheat the oven to 200°C/gas mark 6. Combine the oil, lemon zest and juice, oregano, rosemary and basil in a small bowl.

2] Place the chicken, breast-side up, in a large roasting tin, about 25 x 30cm. Pull back the skin over the breasts (being careful not to tear the skin) and spread the herb mixture over the flesh under the skin. Tuck in the bay leaves and bring the skin back over the flesh. Season the outside of the chicken with salt and pepper.

3] Pour 150ml of water into the tin. Roast the chicken for about 2 hours, basting occasionally. If the water evaporates, add a splash more.

4] Meanwhile, about 40 minutes before the chicken is done, put the potatoes and onion in another roasting tin, about 25 x 30cm. Sprinkle over the thyme and drizzle over the oil. Using your hands, mix thoroughly, ensuring that the potatoes are coated with the oil. Season with salt. Roast for 45 minutes, turning halfway.

5] When the chicken is done (check by inserting a small, sharp knife into the thickest part of the thigh; if the juices run clear, the bird is cooked), remove it from the oven. Transfer it to a board, cover loosely with foil and leave to rest for 10–15 minutes before carving. Pour the cooking juices into a warm jug. Serve the chicken with the potatoes and the juices poured over.

CHARGRILLED CHICKEN WITH GARLIC & ROSEMARY POTATOES

POLLO ALLA GRIGLIA CON PATATE ALL'AGLIO E ROSMARINO

I made this delicious chargrilled chicken dish when we were filming on the wonderful island of Elba, off the coast of Tuscany. There I had the privilege of meeting octogenarian Roberto, who's been studying and working with bees for over 40 years. He taught me how to 'whisper' to the bees and I managed to harvest some fresh honey straight from the hive. I then rubbed it over the meat for added flavour before chargrilling. This is a great way to cook chicken, and the garlic and rosemary potatoes make a wonderful accompaniment.

Serves 4

1.3kg whole free-range chicken
3 tablespoons runny honey
1 tablespoon fresh chopped rosemary
2 garlic cloves, peeled and crushed
3 tablespoons tomato purée
50ml extra virgin olive oil
Juice of ½ lemon
1 tablespoon chopped fresh parsley to garnish
Salt and freshly ground black pepper

For the potatoes
500g new potatoes, scrubbed and halved
75ml extra virgin olive oil
4 garlic cloves, peeled and finely sliced
3 sprigs of rosemary, leaves removed

1] To spatchcock the chicken, remove any trussing string and place the bird breast-side down on a board. Using a sharp knife or poultry shears, cut along both sides of the backbone and discard. Turn the chicken over and, using the heel of your hand, press firmly along the breastbone to break it and flatten the bird.

2] Drizzle the honey over the chicken then scatter over the rosemary and garlic. Spread over the tomato purée and drizzle with oil. Season with salt and pepper. Rub the mixture all over the chicken to coat.

3] Preheat a large ridged cast-iron chargrill pan over a high heat for 5–10 minutes. Once hot, reduce the heat to medium and place the chicken breast-side up on the griddle. Squeeze over the lemon juice. Cook for 15 minutes each side or until golden and cooked through. Leave to rest and keep warm.

4] Meanwhile, bring a pan of salted water to the boil. Parboil the potatoes for 4–5 minutes or until tender and drain thoroughly.

5] Heat the oil in a large frying pan over a medium heat. Add the garlic and as soon as it starts to sizzle add the rosemary and potatoes. Season with salt and pepper. Fry the potatoes for 4–5 minutes or until golden brown, turning often.

6] Cut the chicken into pieces and place on a serving platter with the potatoes. Scatter over the parsley.

I could happily eat pasta every day — and many people in Italy do just that. There are so many different kinds of varying shapes and sizes, and such a vast array of pasta sauces, the possibilities are endless. For centuries, pasta was eaten only in central and southern Italy — in some northern regions it didn't become popular until the 20th century — but today it is the staple food all over Italy. One of the great pasta specialities on the coast is spaghetti vongole, made with clams. I cooked it when we were filming in the Bay of Naples and have included the recipe here. Other popular Italian staples are gnocchi (small dumplings) and risotto, which both originate in northern Italy but are now found throughout the country. Many serve them as a first course or an accompaniment, but I love them as a meal in their own right.

PASTA, GNOCCHI & RISOTTO

LINGUINE WITH PESTO, GREEN BEANS & CAPERS

FETTUCCINE WITH NEAPOLITAN RAGÙ

FETTUCCINE WITH NEAPOLITAN SAUSAGES, MUSHROOMS & PEAS

SPAGHETTI WITH SALAMI & COURGETTE IN A RICH, CREAMY SAUCE

SPAGHETTI WITH CLAMS & MUSSELS

FUSILLI WITH VEGETABLES, PANCETTA, PESTO & MOZZARELLA

PRAWN & RICOTTA RAVIOLI WITH OLIVE OIL & FRESH SAGE

POTATO GNOCCHI WITH COURGETTES & TOMATOES

RICOTTA GNOCCHI WITH RED PEPPERS, COURGETTES, BUTTER & SAGE

SAFFRON RISOTTO WITH PEAS

CHICKEN RISOTTO WITH RED PESTO & ROSEMARY

LINGUINE WITH PESTO, GREEN BEANS & CAPERS

LINGUINE CON PESTO, FAGIOLINI VERDI E CAPPERI

This is a great vegetarian pasta dish that makes a nice change from regular pesto. I created it when filming on the beautiful green, fertile Aeolian island of Salina, which is famous for its capers. For added piquancy, squeeze excess water from the capers into your pasta water.

Serves 4

170ml extra virgin olive oil, plus extra for
  drizzling
1 large garlic clove, peeled and halved
50g pine nuts
60g large fresh basil leaves

70g freshly grated pecorino cheese
50g capers, drained and chopped
500g dried linguine
150g fine green beans, trimmed and halved
Salt and freshly ground black pepper

1] First make the pesto sauce. Put the oil, garlic and pine nuts in a food processor. Blitz for about 1 minute or until the garlic and pine nuts have broken into really small pieces. Add the basil and blitz until smooth. Transfer the mixture to a large bowl. Stir in the pecorino and capers. Season with salt and pepper and set aside.

2] Cook the linguine in a large pan of boiling, salted water until al dente. About 2 minutes before the end of the cooking time, drop in the beans. Reserve 4 tablespoons of the cooking water. Drain the pasta and beans thoroughly.

3] Tip the pasta and beans into the pesto and add the reserved cooking water. Stir gently for about 30 seconds, drizzle over a little extra oil then serve.

FETTUCCINE WITH NEAPOLITAN RAGÙ

FETTUCCINE AL RAGÙ NAPOLETANO

This Neapolitan ragù recipe has been in my family for over 40 years and my mother has never changed a single ingredient. It works to perfection, and the great thing is that you can prepare the sauce a day ahead and it will taste even better the day after. The meat should be crumbly and as soft as butter. Feel free to use rump steak if you prefer, as fillet steak can be expensive.

Serves 6

4 tablespoons olive oil
1 large red onion, peeled and finely chopped
1 large carrot, peeled and finely chopped
1 celery stick, finely chopped
500g fillet steak, cut into 2cm cubes
300ml full-bodied red wine
100ml hot beef stock

4 tablespoons tomato purée
1 x 680g bottle of passata (sieved tomatoes)
10 fresh basil leaves, shredded
500g dried fettuccine
80g freshly grated Parmesan cheese
Salt and freshly ground black pepper

1] Heat the oil in a medium saucepan over a medium heat. Add the onion, carrot and celery and fry for 8–10 minutes, stirring occasionally.

2] Add the steak and fry for 2 minutes. Pour in the wine and let it simmer for about 2 minutes. Season with salt and pepper. Cover and simmer for 30 minutes, stirring occasionally.

3] Stir in the stock, tomato purée and passata. Bring to the boil. Reduce the heat, re-cover and simmer for 1½ hours, stirring every 20 minutes. Stir in the basil and check for seasoning.

4] Cook the fettuccine in a large pan of boiling, salted water until al dente. Drain the pasta thoroughly and tip it back into the same pan.

5] Pour over the sauce and stir for 30 seconds to allow the flavours to combine. Sprinkle the Parmesan over the top before serving.

FETTUCCINE WITH NEAPOLITAN SAUSAGES, MUSHROOMS & PEAS

FETTUCCINE CON SALSICCE NAPOLETANE, FUNGHI E PISELLI

If you want a hearty, meaty pasta dish on the table within half an hour, this one is for you. The main differences between British sausages and Italian *salsicce* is that Italian sausages are all meat, and in a natural casing. They are also slightly coarser (the meat is cut by hand) and more highly seasoned. Each region has its own type of sausage – generally, the further south you go the spicier the flavour. If you can't find Neapolitan sausages use any other Italian sausages, or buy good-quality British ones with a high meat content and season really well.

Serves 4

6 tablespoons olive oil
1 leek, halved lengthways and finely sliced
100g chestnut mushrooms, sliced
2 tablespoons chopped fresh rosemary
400g Neapolitan sausages or good-quality pork sausages, skin removed

100g frozen peas, defrosted
100ml dry white wine
150ml double cream
500g fresh egg fettuccine
80g freshly grated Parmesan cheese
Salt and freshly ground black pepper

1] Heat the oil in a large frying pan over a medium heat. Add the leek, mushrooms and rosemary and fry for 3 minutes, stirring occasionally.

2] Add the sausage meat and fry for 8–10 minutes, breaking it up with a wooden spoon as you go.

3] Stir in the peas and wine. Let the wine bubble for 2 minutes. Pour in the cream, stir well and simmer for 1 minute. Season with salt and pepper. Set aside.

4] Cook the pasta in a large pan of boiling, salted water until al dente. Drain thoroughly and tip it back into the pan.

5] Pour over the sauce and add half the Parmesan. Stir together for 30 seconds to allow the flavours to combine. Transfer to a warm serving bowl and sprinkle over the remaining Parmesan.

SPAGHETTI WITH SALAMI & COURGETTE IN A RICH, CREAMY SAUCE

SPAGHETTI CON SALAME PICCANTE

I love the contrast of the spicy salami with the creaminess of the eggs and cheese in this recipe, and the courgette adds flavour, colour and a soft texture. You can use any pecorino (sheep's milk cheese) for this recipe, but I particularly like pecorino sardo (from Sardinia), as it has a wonderful salty, piquant flavour. If you prefer, use peas instead of courgettes. As with spaghetti carbonara, the heat from the pasta will cook the egg.

5 tablespoons olive oil
1 large courgette, trimmed and cut into
 1cm cubes
200g sliced spicy salami, cut into strips
30g salted butter
4 medium eggs

½ teaspoon freshly ground black pepper
4 tablespoons chopped fresh flat-leaf parsley
4 tablespoons full-fat milk
80g freshly grated pecorino cheese
500g dried spaghetti
Salt

Serves 4

1] Heat the oil in a medium frying pan over a medium heat. Add the courgette and salami and fry for 6 minutes, stirring occasionally. Stir in the butter. Remove from the heat.

2] Crack the eggs into a bowl. Add the pepper, parsley, milk and half the pecorino. Season with salt and set aside.

3] Cook the pasta in a large pan of boiling, salted water until al dente. Drain the pasta thoroughly and tip it back into the same pan. Working quickly off the heat, add the egg and the salami and courgette mixture. Stir for 30 seconds to combine.

4] Transfer to a warm serving bowl and sprinkle over the remaining pecorino.

SPAGHETTI WITH CLAMS & MUSSELS

SPAGHETTI VONGOLE

As a young man I often used to go to the pretty port town of Castellammare, near Naples, to eat platefuls of their famous mussels. When I found myself there again recently, filming *Gino's Italian Coastal Escape*, I couldn't resist making the classic dish of the region – the chilli-spiked spaghetti vongole. Traditionally, spaghetti vongole contains just clams, but as I was in Castellammare, of course I had to include some mussels.

Serves 2

250g live clams
150g live mussels
1 garlic clove, peeled and finely sliced
1 fresh, medium-hot red chilli, finely sliced
3 tablespoons olive oil

150ml dry white wine
3 tablespoons chopped fresh flat-leaf parsley
300g dried spaghetti
12 yellow cherry tomatoes, quartered
Salt

1] Prepare the clams and mussels (see page 70, steps 1 and 2). Bring a large pan of salted water to the boil.

2] Meanwhile, put the garlic and chilli in a large saucepan or wok. Add the oil and place the pan over a medium heat. As soon as the garlic starts to sizzle, add the clams and mussels.

3] Pour in the wine and stir in the parsley. Bring to the boil, cover and cook for about 5–7 minutes or until the mussels have opened. Discard any mussels that remain closed.

4] Meanwhile, cook the spaghetti in the boiling water until al dente. Drain the pasta and tip it into the pan with the clams and mussels. Add the tomatoes and cook for 1 minute, stirring. Tip onto a large serving plate and serve immediately.

FUSILLI WITH VEGETABLES, PANCETTA, PESTO & MOZZARELLA

FUSILLI CON VERDURE, PANCETTA, MOZZARELLA E PESTO

When I was filming in southern Campania, in the medieval town of Felitto, I met the wonderful Rosy – the 'First Lady' of fusilli lunghi (long pasta spirals). She still makes fusilli the traditional way, hand-rolling individual lengths of dough around a square wire to make a long, gently twisty thread of pasta with a small hole in it. As a thank you to her for showing me her techniques, I made this pasta sauce from the locally produced fresh vegetables and mozzarella that the region is so famous for. If you can't find fusilli lunghi in the shops, use any long pasta such as spaghetti, linguine or bucatini.

100ml olive oil
1 large aubergine, cut into 1cm cubes
1 large courgette, cut into 1cm cubes
2 medium red onions, peeled and finely sliced
150g diced pancetta
2 x 400g tins of cherry tomatoes

2 tablespoons fresh or shop-bought basil pesto
500g dried fusilli lunghi
2 x 125g balls of mozzarella cheese, drained and cut into small cubes
Salt and freshly ground black pepper

Serves 6

1] Heat the oil in a large frying pan over a medium heat. Add the aubergine and courgette and some salt and fry for 7–8 minutes. Add the onions and pancetta and fry for 8 minutes.

2] Stir in the tomatoes and pesto. Simmer for 15 minutes, stirring occasionally. Season with salt and pepper and set aside.

3] Cook the fusilli lunghi in a large pan of boiling, salted water until al dente. Drain the pasta thoroughly and tip it back into the same saucepan you cooked it in. Pour over the sauce. Stir to combine.

4] Return the pan to a low heat. Add the mozzarella and stir until it starts to melt and go stringy. Serve immediately.

PRAWN & RICOTTA RAVIOLI WITH OLIVE OIL & FRESH SAGE

RAVIOLI DI GAMBERONI E RICOTTA CON OLIO DI OLIVA E SALVIA

Ravioli are popular all over Italy, stuffed with a variety of different ingredients depending on the region and the season. Wherever you are on the coast, you'll usually find them filled with seafood, as in this recipe.

Serves 4

400g '00' grade pasta flour, plus extra for dusting
½ teaspoon fine salt
2 teaspoons very finely ground black pepper
2 egg yolks
3 medium eggs, lightly beaten
230ml extra virgin olive oil
8 large (or 16 medium) fresh sage leaves
½ teaspoon grated lemon zest, to serve

For the filling
750g ricotta cheese
Grated zest of 2 unwaxed lemons
250g cooked king prawns, peeled and finely chopped
3 tablespoons chopped fresh chives
2 medium eggs, lightly beaten
Salt

1] First make the dough: place the flour, salt and pepper in a large bowl. Make a well in the centre and add the egg yolks, beaten eggs and 2 tablespoons of the oil. Using the handle of a wooden spoon, gradually mix the flour into the liquid. Once the texture is crumbly, turn out the mixture onto a well-floured surface.

2] Knead for about 8–10 minutes until you have a soft, smooth dough. The technique is the same as for bread: hold the dough in one hand and fold, push down and stretch the dough away from you with the other hand. Rotate and repeat. Shape the dough into a ball, wrap in cling film and chill for 30 minutes. Meanwhile, put the ricotta, lemon zest, prawns and chives in a large bowl and mix with a fork. Cover with cling film and refrigerate for at least 15 minutes.

3] Remove the cling film from the dough, dust the dough lightly with flour and cut into 2 even-sized pieces. Roll out each piece to about 2mm thick, either using a pasta machine or a rolling pin (dust the rolling pin and work surface with flour first). Dust frequently with flour or the dough can become sticky.

4] Lay 1 piece of dough on a well-dusted work surface. Place a tablespoonful of the filling on the dough and repeat at 5cm intervals over half the sheet only. Lightly brush the spaces around the filling with the 2 beaten eggs. Fold over the dough to cover the filling. Press gently around each spoonful of filling to expel the air. Using a 5.5cm round ravioli stamp cutter, cut out the ravioli. Cover with a tea towel and repeat with the other piece of dough.

5] Cook the ravioli in a large pan of boiling, salted water for 3 minutes. Meanwhile, heat the remaining oil in a large frying pan over a medium heat. Add the sage. As soon as it starts to sizzle, transfer the ravioli using a slotted spoon to the pan with the sage. Gently toss to coat. To serve, sprinkle over a little lemon zest.

POTATO GNOCCHI WITH COURGETTES & TOMATOES

GNOCCHI DI PATATE CON ZUCCHINE E POMODORI

Gnocchi are most commonly made with potatoes but there are many regional variations, so depending on where you are in Italy you'll also find them containing pumpkin, polenta, rice, semolina or ricotta (see page 144); there are even sweet gnocchi in some areas. This is a lovely light recipe for summer, when tomatoes and courgettes are in season.

Serves 4

600g floury potatoes, such as Desirée or Maris Piper, peeled and cut into 5cm chunks
200g plain flour or '00' grade pasta flour, plus extra for dusting
1½ teaspoons salt, plus extra for seasoning
½ teaspoon freshly ground black pepper, plus extra for seasoning
2 medium eggs, lightly beaten

50g salted butter
5 tablespoons extra virgin olive oil
2 medium courgettes, cut into 1cm cubes
3 large fresh plum tomatoes, deseeded and cut into 1cm cubes
60g freshly grated Parmesan cheese
8 large basil leaves, shredded

1] Put the potatoes in a large pan and cover with cold, salted water. Bring to the boil then simmer for 15–20 minutes or until tender. Drain well and leave for 2–3 minutes. Pass the potatoes through a potato ricer set over a large bowl or mash until really smooth. While the potatoes are still warm, add the flour and salt and pepper. Make a well and add the eggs. Using the handle of a wooden spoon, mix thoroughly then turn out onto a floured surface. Knead lightly until you have soft, slightly sticky dough. (Do not overwork or the dough will be tough.)

2] Divide the dough into 4. Roll each piece with your hands into a long sausage shape, about 1.5cm thick. Use a sharp knife to cut across into 2cm lengths. Lay the gnocchi on a lightly floured clean tea towel or tray until ready to cook.

3] Bring a large pan of salted water to the boil. Meanwhile, heat the butter and oil in a large frying pan over a high heat. Add the courgettes and fry for 5 minutes, stirring occasionally. Season with some salt and pepper. Remove the pan from the heat and set aside.

4] Drop the gnocchi into the boiling water and cook for about 2–3 minutes. They will be ready when they float to the surface. Drain thoroughly.

5] Return the frying pan to the heat and tip in the gnocchi. Stir in the tomatoes, half the Parmesan and the basil and fry for 1 minute, stirring continuously. Sprinkle over the remaining Parmesan and serve immediately.

RICOTTA GNOCCHI WITH RED PEPPERS, COURGETTES, BUTTER & SAGE

NDUNDERI CON PEPERONI ROSSI, ZUCCHINE, BURRO E SALVIA

When I was filming recently in Minori – one of the gems of the Amalfi coast – I met expert pasta-maker Claudia, who taught me how to prepare the regional speciality, ndunderi. It's a ricotta and flour-based gnocchi and is named for the sound the pasta makes when it hits your plate. I've dressed the gnocchi in butter, sage and Parmesan – a classic Italian combination – and added red peppers and courgettes for extra flavour, colour and texture. It is important to drain the ricotta the day before or the gnocchi will be soggy and not hold together properly.

Serves 4

400g ricotta cheese
4 egg yolks
60g freshly grated Parmesan cheese
2 teaspoons salt
1 teaspoon ground black pepper
½ teaspoon freshly grated nutmeg
160g '00' grade pasta flour

For the sauce
150ml extra virgin olive oil
2 medium courgettes, cut into 5mm cubes
2 large red peppers, cut into 5mm cubes
8 large fresh sage leaves, shredded
100g salted butter
60g freshly grated Parmesan cheese
Salt and freshly ground black pepper

1] Put the ricotta in a piece of muslin or a clean tea towel and place in a colander. Leave to drain overnight.

2] In a medium bowl, combine the ricotta, egg yolks, Parmesan, salt, pepper and nutmeg. Add the flour. Using the handle of a wooden spoon, gradually mix together thoroughly.

3] Use your hands to bring the dough together into a ball and place on a lightly floured work surface. Divide the dough into 4. Roll each piece beneath the palms of your hands into a long sausage shape, each about 2.5cm thick. Use a sharp knife to cut across into 2.5cm lengths. Dust with a little flour. Press each piece against the tines of a fork to create small grooves on one side. Place the gnocchi on a lightly floured tray or tea towel until ready to cook.

4] To make the sauce, heat the oil in a large frying pan over a high heat. Add the courgettes, red peppers and some salt and fry for about 7 minutes, stirring occasionally. Add the sage and butter, stirring until the butter has melted and everything is well combined. Remove the pan from the heat and set aside.

5] Bring a large pan of salted water to the boil. Drop the gnocchi into the boiling water and cook for about 5 minutes. Once they have floated to the surface, continue to cook for 2 further minutes. Remove the gnocchi with a slotted spoon and stir them into the sauce. Return the frying pan to the heat for 1 minute. Add some black pepper and sprinkle over the Parmesan.

SAFFRON RISOTTO WITH PEAS

RISOTTO ZAFFERANO E PISELLI

This simple risotto is perfect for lunchtime entertaining or a light supper. The saffron gives the dish its wonderful rich golden colour and distinctive flavour, and the peas provide sweetness and contrast in texture and colour. The best saffron in southern Italy comes from Sicily, where they use it in both savoury and sweet dishes. I know it's a bit expensive, but you only need to use a tiny amount and it's worth every penny.

½ teaspoon saffron threads
1.3 litres hot vegetable stock
6 tablespoons olive oil
1 large onion, peeled and finely chopped
400g Arborio or Carnaroli rice

150ml dry rosé or white wine
80g salted butter
200g frozen petit pois, defrosted
80g freshly grated Grana Padano cheese
Salt and white pepper

Olives 4

1] Put the saffron in a small bowl with 4 tablespoons of the stock and set aside to infuse. Meanwhile, heat the olive oil in a large, heavy-based saucepan over a medium heat. Add the onion and fry for 5 minutes or until softened but not browned, stirring occasionally.

2] Add the rice and fry for 3 minutes, stirring constantly, or until the grains are coated and shiny.

3] Pour in the wine and let it bubble for 1 minute or until it has evaporated.

4] Stir in the saffron mixture. Add 2 ladlesful of stock and bring to a simmer. Stir continuously until the liquid has been absorbed. Continue adding the rest of the stock in the same way, until the rice is cooked but still has a slight bite. This will take 16–18 minutes and you may not need to add all the stock.

5] Remove the pan from the heat. Add the butter, peas and Grana Padano and stir for about 30 seconds until creamy. Season with salt and pepper.

CHICKEN RISOTTO WITH RED PESTO & ROSEMARY

RISOTTO CON POLLO, PESTO ROSSO E ROSMARINO

Risotto is the ultimate comfort food, and it's so versatile and quick to make. For this recipe I've used chicken breast, but you can also use cooked chicken left over from a roast – just stir it in as you add the last ladleful of stock. Red pesto is a southern Italian variation of the northern Italian basil pesto – the colour comes from sun-dried tomatoes or red peppers and the sauce adds depth of flavour and piquancy to this dish.

8 tablespoons olive oil
1 large red onion, peeled and finely chopped
250g skinless boneless chicken breast, cut into 2cm cubes
1 tablespoon chopped fresh rosemary
400g Arborio or Carnaroli rice
150ml dry white wine
1.3 litres hot vegetable stock

50g salted butter
2 tablespoons shop-bought red, sun-dried tomato pesto
50g freshly grated Parmesan cheese
50g Parmesan cheese shavings
Extra virgin olive oil for drizzling
Salt and freshly ground black pepper

Serves 4

1] Heat 4 tablespoons of the oil in a large, heavy-based saucepan over a medium heat. Add the onion and fry for 5 minutes until softened but not browned. Add the chicken and rosemary and fry for a further 5 minutes, stirring occasionally. Using a slotted spoon, transfer the chicken and onion to a plate. Cover with foil and set aside.

2] Heat the remaining 4 tablespoons of oil in the same pan. When hot, add the rice and fry for 3 minutes, stirring continuously, until the rice is well coated in the oil. Pour in the wine and let it simmer for 1 minute or until it has evaporated.

3] Pour in 2 ladlesful of stock and bring to a simmer. Stir continuously until the liquid has been absorbed. Continue adding the rest of the stock in the same way, until the rice is cooked but still has a slight bite. This will take 16–18 minutes and you may not need to add all the stock.

4] Take the pan off the heat. Return the chicken and onion to the pan, then stir in the butter, red pesto and grated Parmesan. Stir gently for 30 seconds. Season with salt and pepper. Scatter Parmesan shavings over the top and drizzle over some extra virgin olive oil.

I love making pizza and bread — it's so satisfying, the results are incredible and it's a lot easier than you might think. You can be as creative as you like — once you've got the dough right, more or less anything goes. Here I've included pizzas with seafood toppings, which you'll find along the coast, and have adapted traditional Neapolitan recipes that use simple local ingredients such as buffalo mozzarella and plum tomatoes. My favourite recipe in this chapter has to be my father's calzone — if you like spicy flavours, this one is for you. Among the breads are the familiar and popular ciabatta and focaccia, but I've also included a stuffed focaccia and some sweet rolls, which are a little more unusual and absolutely delicious.

PIZZA & BREADS

NEAPOLITAN PIZZA WITH BUFFALO MOZZARELLA, TOMATOES & BASIL

TOMATO, GARLIC & OREGANO PIZZA

PIZZA TRAY WITH SMOKED SALMON, MASCARPONE & MOZZARELLA

SEAFOOD PIZZA

PIZZA TRAY WITH ANCHOVIES, COURGETTES, GARLIC & CHILLI

PAPA CIRO'S SPICY CALZONE

SWEET SOFT BUTTER ROLLS WITH VANILLA

FOCACCIA WITH TOMATOES, OLIVES, CAPERS & RED PESTO

FOCACCIA STUFFED WITH GORGONZOLA, OLIVES, GARLIC & ROSEMARY

OLIVE & FENNEL SEED CIABATTA

NEAPOLITAN PIZZA WITH BUFFALO MOZZARELLA, TOMATOES & BASIL

PIZZA MARGHERITA

Pizza originated in Naples and it's where the best, most authentic pizza can still be found today – and I'm not just saying that because I'm a Neapolitan! Apparently this topping was created in the 19th century to honour the visit of Queen Margherita to Naples, as it represented the colours of the Italian flag – red, white and green. Try to use buffalo (rather than cow's milk) mozzarella if you can.

Makes 2

200g strong white flour, plus extra for dusting
1 x 7g sachet of fast-action (easy-blend) dried yeast
½ teaspoon salt
2 tablespoons extra virgin olive oil, plus extra for greasing and brushing

For the topping
1 x 400g tin of chopped tomatoes
2 tablespoons extra virgin olive oil
2 x 125g balls of buffalo mozzarella cheese, drained and cut into small cubes
10 fresh basil leaves
Salt and freshly ground black pepper

1] Put the flour in a large bowl. Add the yeast to one side of the bowl and the salt to the other. Make a well in the centre and add the oil then gradually pour in 140ml warm water. Using the handle of a wooden spoon, mix together thoroughly to create a wet dough. Turn out the dough onto a well-floured surface and knead it for about 5 minutes or until smooth and elastic.

2] Shape the dough into a round and place in a large oiled bowl. Brush the top with a little oil and cover with cling film. Leave to rest at room temperature for 20–25 minutes. Preheat the oven to 220°C/gas mark 7.

3] Meanwhile, make the topping. Put the tomatoes, oil, salt and pepper in a small bowl. Using your hands, squeeze the tomatoes to make a fine pulp. Set aside.

4] Turn out the dough onto a lightly floured surface and knead just 3 or 4 times to knock out the air. Halve the dough and place each half in the centre of an oiled baking sheet. Use your fingertips to push each half out from the centre, stretching the dough to create 2 rounds about 25cm in diameter and 1–2cm thick. You can also use a rolling pin if you prefer. Make a small rim by pulling up the edges slightly.

5] Spread the tomato mixture evenly over the pizza bases, avoiding the rim, and top with the mozzarella. Bake for 12–14 minutes or until golden brown.

6] Remove from the oven, scatter over the basil and return to the oven for 1 further minute.

TOMATO, GARLIC & OREGANO PIZZA

PIZZA AL POMODORO, AGLIO E ORIGANO

Simple, tasty and light – this is how a good pizza should be. Always use the best-quality ingredients you can afford, as it will really make a difference to the flavour. In Naples we would use San Marzano tomatoes – a type of plum tomato that grows in the volcanic soil around Mount Vesuvius and has a rich, sweet flavour and dense texture. You can buy tinned San Marzano tomatoes in Britain, but if you can't find them another really good-quality brand of plum tomato will be fine. You can add a few anchovies on top if you like, but generally it's best to keep things simple.

Makes 2

200g strong white flour, plus extra for dusting
1 x 7g sachet of fast-action (easy-blend)
  dried yeast
½ teaspoon salt
2 tablespoons extra virgin olive oil, plus extra
  for greasing and brushing

For the topping
1 x 400g tin of chopped tomatoes
2 tablespoons extra virgin olive oil
4 garlic cloves, peeled and finely chopped
1 teaspoon dried oregano
Salt and freshly ground black pepper

1] Put the flour in a large bowl. Add the yeast to one side of the bowl and the salt to the other. Make a well in the centre and add the oil then gradually pour in 140ml warm water. Using the handle of a wooden spoon, mix together thoroughly to create a wet dough. Turn out the dough onto a well-floured surface and knead it for about 5 minutes or until smooth and elastic.

2] Shape the dough into a round and place in a large oiled bowl. Brush the top with a little oil and cover with cling film. Leave to rest at room temperature for 20–25 minutes. Preheat the oven to 220°C/gas mark 7.

3] Meanwhile, make the topping. Put the tomatoes in a small bowl with the oil, salt and pepper. Using your hands, squeeze the tomatoes to make a fine pulp. Set aside.

4] Turn out the dough onto a lightly floured surface and knead just 3 or 4 times to knock out the air. Halve the dough and place each half in the centre of an oiled baking sheet. Use your fingertips to push each half out from the centre, stretching the dough to create 2 rounds about 25cm in diameter and 1–2cm thick. You can also use a rolling pin if you prefer. Make a small rim by pulling up the edges slightly.

5] Spread the tomato mixture evenly over the pizza bases, avoiding the rim. Scatter over the garlic. Bake for 14 minutes or until golden brown. Remove from the oven, sprinkle over the oregano and bake for 1 further minute.

PIZZA TRAY WITH SMOKED SALMON, MASCARPONE & MOZZARELLA

TEGLIA DI PIZZA CON MASCARPONE E SALMONE AFFUMICATO

The first time I tried this pizza topping was on the island of Elba, off the coast of Tuscany. It isn't traditional, but the combination of smoked salmon, soft creamy cheeses and chives works really well and I was seriously impressed. If you've never made homemade pizza before, a pizza tray is probably a good introduction, as you don't have to worry about creating the perfect round pizza shape.

200g strong white flour, plus extra for dusting
1 x 7g sachet of fast-action (easy-blend) dried yeast
½ teaspoon salt
2 tablespoons extra virgin olive oil, plus extra for greasing and brushing

For the topping
250g mascarpone cheese (room temperature)
4 tablespoons full-fat milk
2 tablespoons chopped fresh chives
1 x 125g ball of mozzarella cheese, drained and cut into small cubes
120g smoked salmon trimmings, roughly sliced
Salt and freshly ground black pepper

Serves 2

1] Put the flour in a large bowl. Add the yeast to one side of the bowl and the salt to the other. Make a well in the centre and add the oil then gradually pour in 140ml warm water. Using the handle of a wooden spoon, mix together thoroughly to create a wet dough. Turn out the dough onto a well-floured surface and knead for about 5 minutes or until smooth and elastic.

2] Shape the dough into a round and place in a large oiled bowl. Brush the top with a little oil and cover with cling film. Leave to rest at room temperature for 20–25 minutes.

3] To make the topping, put the mascarpone in a medium bowl and pour over the milk. Add the chives, season with salt and pepper and mix with a fork until smooth. Set aside.

4] Turn out the dough onto a lightly floured surface and knead just 3 or 4 times to knock out the air. Transfer to an oiled traybake tin, about 25 x 23cm and at least 2cm high. Using your fingertips, gently flatten the dough to extend to the sides (it should be about 1cm thick). Brush over a little oil, cover with a tea towel and leave to rise again in a warm place for a further 20 minutes. Preheat the oven to 220°C/gas mark 7.

5] Spread the mascarpone mixture evenly over the pizza tray base, leaving a 1cm border clear. Scatter over the mozzarella and bake for 12 minutes. Remove from the oven, scatter over the smoked salmon and bake for a further 3 minutes.

SEAFOOD PIZZA

PIZZA CON VONGOLE E COZZE

In summer there is an abundance of mussels and clams along the southern Italian coast and they're used frequently as pizza toppings. If you have the good fortune to visit the Amalfi coast you'll find this in most pizzerias.

Makes 2

200g strong white flour, plus extra for dusting
1 x 7g sachet of fast-action (easy-blend) dried yeast
½ teaspoon salt
2 tablespoons extra virgin olive oil, plus extra for greasing and brushing

For the topping
500g live clams
500g live mussels
4 tablespoons extra virgin olive oil
50ml dry white wine
1 x 400g tin of chopped tomatoes
4 garlic cloves, peeled and finely chopped
2 tablespoons fresh chopped flat-leaf parsley
Salt and freshly ground black pepper

1] To make the topping, first prepare the clams and mussels (see page 70, steps 1 and 2). Heat 2 tablespoons of the oil in a large saucepan over a high heat. Add the clams, mussels and wine. Cover the pan and cook for 5 minutes, shaking the pan every minute or so. Remove from the heat and leave to rest for 20 minutes. Meanwhile, put the tomatoes, remaining 2 tablespoons of oil and salt and pepper in a small bowl. Using your hands, squeeze the tomatoes to make a fine pulp. Remove the clams and mussels from their shells (discard the shells). Set aside.

2] Put the flour in a large bowl. Add the yeast to one side of the bowl and the salt to the other. Make a well in the centre and add the oil then gradually pour in 140ml warm water. Using the handle of a wooden spoon, mix to create a wet dough. Turn out the dough onto a well-floured surface and knead for 5 minutes or until smooth and elastic. Shape the dough into a round and place in a large oiled bowl. Brush the top with a little oil and cover with cling film. Leave to rest at room temperature for 20–25 minutes. Preheat the oven to 220°C/gas mark 7.

3] Turn out the dough onto a lightly floured surface and knead just 3 or 4 times to knock out the air. Halve the dough and place each half in the centre of an oiled baking sheet. Use your fingertips to push each half out from the centre, stretching the dough to create 2 rounds about 25cm in diameter and 1–2cm thick. You can also use a rolling pin if you prefer. Make a small rim by pulling up the edges slightly.

4] Spread the tomato mixture evenly over the pizza bases, avoiding the rim. Scatter over the garlic and bake for 12 minutes. Remove from the oven, scatter over the clams and mussels and return to the oven for 3 minutes. Sprinkle over the parsley.

PIZZA TRAY WITH ANCHOVIES, COURGETTES, GARLIC & CHILLI

TEGLIA DI PIZZA PICCANTE CON ACCIUGHE, ZUCCHINE, E AGLIO

Anchovies are found in large numbers in the Mediterranean, particularly in southern Italy, where they are a staple food and are eaten fresh or preserved in olive oil or salt. They're high in antioxidants, and some research suggests they may be linked to longevity. If you prefer, replace the anchovies with black olives.

Serves 2

200g strong white flour, plus extra for dusting
1 x 7g sachet fast-action (easy-blend) dried yeast
½ teaspoon salt
2 tablespoons extra virgin olive oil, plus extra for greasing and brushing

For the topping
6 tablespoons oil
2 large courgettes, cut into 1cm cubes
1 x 400g tin of chopped tomatoes
½ teaspoon dried chilli flakes
4 garlic cloves, peeled and finely chopped
16 anchovy fillets in oil, drained
1 teaspoon dried oregano
Salt

1] Put the flour in a large bowl. Add the yeast to one side of the bowl and the salt to the other. Make a well in the centre and add the oil then gradually pour in 140ml warm water. Using the handle of a wooden spoon, mix together thoroughly to create a wet dough. Turn out the dough onto a well-floured surface and knead for about 5 minutes or until smooth and elastic. Shape the dough into a round and place in a large oiled bowl. Brush the top with a little oil and cover with cling film. Leave to rest at room temperature for 20–25 minutes.

2] Meanwhile, make the topping. Heat 4 tablespoons of the oil in a medium pan over a medium heat. Add the courgettes, season with salt and fry for 12 minutes, stirring occasionally. Leave to cool. Put the tomatoes in a small bowl with the remaining 2 tablespoons of the oil, the salt and the chilli flakes. Using your hands (you may want to use gloves to protect your hands and eyes from the chilli), squeeze the tomatoes to create a fine pulp. Set aside.

3] Turn out the dough onto a lightly floured surface and knead just 3 or 4 times to knock out the air. Transfer to an oiled traybake tin, about 25 x 23cm and at least 2cm high. Using your fingertips, gently flatten the dough to extend to the sides (it should be about 1cm thick). Brush over a little oil, cover with a tea towel and leave to rise again in a warm place for a further 20 minutes. Preheat the oven to 220°C/gas mark 7.

4] Remove the tea towel and spread the tomato mixture evenly over the pizza base, leaving a 1cm border clear. Scatter over the garlic and cooled courgettes and lay the anchovies on top. Bake for 12–14 minutes or until golden brown. Remove from the oven, sprinkle over the oregano and bake for 1 further minute.

TUSCAN SPECIALITIES

One of the most visited regions in Italy, Tuscany has stunning landscapes that include an extensive coastline, rolling hills and the beautiful neighbouring island of Elba. Generally, Tuscan cuisine is extremely varied, simple and rustic, with its roots in peasant traditions. The raw ingredients are excellent and the flavours strong and punchy, with fresh herbs used widely, but it is the liberal use of olive oil that really defines the food of this region. Soups and meat of all kinds are extremely popular, and bread (often unsalted) is an important staple. Pasta is less popular than in many other regions.

CANNELLINI BEANS

Sometimes referred to as the *mangiafagioli* ('bean eaters'), the Tuscans love their pulses. They are particularly fond of the rich, creamy white cannellini beans (see below). These are often paired with pork and tuna or used in salads, soups and stews, and are sometimes served on their own with sage and garlic. Cannellini beans are a key ingredient of *ribollita* – a classic Tuscan bean soup that contains toasted bread rubbed with garlic.

WILD MUSHROOMS

In Tuscany and on the neighbouring island of Elba, wild mushrooms – particularly the intensely flavoured *porcini* (see below) – grow in abundance in the woods. In autumn, locals rise at dawn to forage for these highly prized delicacies – a tradition that has become a competitive pasttime. Wild mushrooms are served in many ways, sometimes with polenta or risotto, or simply fried in olive oil. A particularly Tuscan method is to sauté them with chicken livers in olive oil flavoured with sage. *Porcini* are often dried, which preserves them and makes their flavour very concentrated in the process.

CHESTNUTS

Although chestnuts (see below) are mainly associated with northern Italy, they also play an important part in the cuisine of Tuscany and the island of Elba. Chestnut trees grow in mountainous regions and the nuts are harvested in the autumn. Tuscany has its own speciality made with chestnuts – *castagnaccio*, which is a cake made with chestnut flour, olive oil, sultanas, pine nuts or walnuts and fennel seeds or rosemary. Its popularity has spread and it is now found throughout Italy.

HONEY

The honey on Elba is arguably the best in Italy – because of the island's great biodiversity, the bees gather nectar from a wide selection of flowers, producing different types of honey, each with its own distinctive flavour and scent. Arbutus honey is perhaps most characteristic of the area, but there is also acacia, wildflower, eucalyptus, rosemary, thistle and chestnut honeys, to name but a few. Honey is used as a sweetener in cooking, but it is also served with cheese at the end of a meal.

OLIVES & OLIVE OIL

Tuscany is well known for its olives (see below), and one of the most distinctive elements of Tuscan cooking is the generous use of olive oil. Although olive oil is produced in 19 out of the 20 regions of Italy, mainly in the south, Tuscan olive oils are considered by many to be some of the best, especially the fruity-flavoured oil from the province of Lucca. Extra virgin olive oil is extracted from the first pressing of the olives and is best for salads and uncooked dishes.

FISH & SHELLFISH

All along the Tuscan coast you'll find wonderful seafood dishes. Grey mullet, cuttlefish and octopus are all popular, as are mussels and clams. The king of Tuscan seafood dishes is *cacciucco* – a chunky seafood soup or stew that originates in Livorno and includes chilli and at least five different types of fish. It is served on slices of toasted bread rubbed with garlic. Elvers (*cieche*), caught at the mouth of the Arno near Pisa, are also a great favourite in Tuscany.

BOTTARGA

Made mainly in Sardinia but also in Orbetello in Tuscany, *bottarga* (see below) is the compressed, salted and dried roe of the grey mullet. It is a magical ingredient and can transform dishes with its intensely savoury, salty flavour. You can grate or shave *bottarga* onto pasta and pizzas, or slice it finely and use it as a topping for toasted ciabatta. It can also be served on its own as an antipasto, sliced and marinated in olive oil and lemon juice. Some *bottarga*, produced mainly in Sicily, is made from the roe of tuna rather than grey mullet.

CHEESE

There is a strong tradition of raising sheep in Tuscany, so many of the cheeses are made from sheep's milk, including *pecorino toscano*, *pecorino di Pienze*, *marzolino del Chianti* and *caciotte*, which is made from a mixture of sheep and cow's milk. The *pecorino* in Tuscany is considered by many to be the best in Italy, and it is often served at the end of a meal. There are also great goat's cheeses from Maremma and Mugello.

WINE

Tuscany is the most established wine-growing region in Italy. Although it doesn't produce the most in terms of quantity, two of Italy's most famous wines are made there: Chianti (in the hills between Florence and Siena) and Brunello di Montalcino (south of Siena). Other quality wines produced in Tuscany include Moscatello di Montalcino, Vernaccia di San Gimignano, Aleatico di Portoferraio and the sweet dessert wine, vin santo.

PAPA CIRO'S SPICY CALZONE

IL CALZONE BRUCIA-CULO DI PAPÀ CIRO

When my late father came to stay with me in London, we were in the kitchen experimenting with different pizzas and toppings and he created this folded pizza filled with peppers, olives, ricotta and chilli. He loved spicy food and was delighted with the results. Be ready for something very special and really hot!

Makes 2

200g strong white flour, plus extra for dusting
1 x 7g sachet of fast-action (easy-blend) dried yeast
½ teaspoon salt
2 tablespoons extra virgin olive oil, plus extra for greasing and brushing
3 tablespoons chilli oil

For the filling
4 tablespoons extra virgin olive oil
1 large red onion, peeled and thinly sliced

1 red pepper, deseeded and sliced into 5mm strips
1 yellow pepper, deseeded and sliced into 5mm strips
1 green pepper, deseeded and sliced into 5mm strips
2 teaspoons dried chilli flakes
100g pitted black olives (preferably Leccino), drained and halved
250g ricotta cheese (room temperature)
Salt

1] To make the filling, heat the oil in a large frying pan over a medium heat. Add the onion, peppers, chilli flakes and some salt and fry for 10 minutes, stirring occasionally. Add the olives and fry for 5 minutes. Set aside. Place the ricotta in a bowl and mash with a fork until smooth, creamy and easy to spread. Set aside.

2] Place the flour in a large bowl. Add the yeast to one side and the salt to the other. Make a well in the centre and add the oil then gradually pour in 140ml warm water. Using the handle of a wooden spoon, mix to create a wet dough. Turn out the dough onto a well-floured surface and knead for about 5 minutes or until smooth and elastic. Shape the dough into a round and place in a large oiled bowl. Brush the top with a little oil and cover with cling film. Leave to rest at room temperature for 20–25 minutes. Preheat the oven to 220°C/gas mark 7.

3] Turn out the dough onto a lightly floured surface and knead just 3 or 4 times to knock out the air. Halve the dough and place each half in the centre of an oiled baking sheet. Use your fingertips to push each half out from the centre, stretching the dough to create 2 rounds about 22cm in diameter.

4] Spread the ricotta evenly over half the surface of each pizza base, leaving a border of 1cm all around, then spoon over the pepper mixture. Fold over the empty side to enclose the filling. Pinch the edges to seal and crimp them by making tucks at regular intervals. Brush the surface with chilli oil and bake for 15 minutes or until golden brown.

SWEET SOFT BUTTER ROLLS WITH VANILLA

BOCCONCINI DI PANE DOLCE AL BURRO E VANIGLIA

These delicious little rolls are the creation of the Neapolitan baker Vincenzo Mennella. I know his son, Liborio, very well and I've been chasing him for this recipe for the last 21 years. Finally he agreed to give it to me, after I made him an offer he couldn't refuse! The rolls are very versatile – they're great served with savoury antipasti such as Italian cured hams and salami, or with sweet preserves such as strawberry jam.

Makes 16
small rolls

450g strong white flour, plus extra for dusting
10g fast-action (easy blend) dried yeast
1 teaspoon salt
60g caster sugar
150g salted butter, melted

120ml warm full-fat milk
3 medium eggs
1 tablespoon vanilla extract
Icing sugar for dusting

1] Combine the flour, yeast, salt and sugar in a large bowl. Make a well in the centre and pour in 50g of the melted butter and the milk. Mix together using the handle of a wooden spoon. Cover with cling film and leave to rest at room temperature for 30 minutes.

2] Break the eggs into a small bowl. Beat lightly with a fork then stir in the vanilla. Add the eggs gradually to the mixture in the larger bowl, pouring in a steady stream and stirring all the time until thoroughly combined.

3] Turn out the dough onto a well-floured surface and knead for 5–10 minutes or until soft and elastic. Brush the inside of a large bowl with melted butter. Shape the dough into a round and place in the bowl. Brush the top with melted butter and cover with cling film. Leave in a warm, draught-free place for 1½ hours or until doubled in size. Brush a 20cm loose-bottomed round or square cake tin with melted butter.

4] Tip the dough out onto a lightly floured surface and knead 3 or 4 times to knock out the air. Cut the dough into 16 equal-sized pieces and shape into balls. Roll the balls in melted butter and place in the cake tin, spacing them slightly apart. Cover with a tea towel and leave to rise in a warm place for about 1 hour or until doubled in size. Preheat the oven to 190°C/gas mark 5.

5] Brush the rolls with the remaining melted butter. Bake for 25 minutes or until golden brown and firm.

6] Leave to cool slightly or completely on a wire rack, then dust with icing sugar and serve.

FOCACCIA WITH TOMATOES, OLIVES, CAPERS & RED PESTO

FOCACCIA CON POMODORINI, OLIVE, CAPPERI E PESTO ROSSO

As I was filming the new series of *Gino's Italian Coastal Escape* along Italy's beautiful Mediterranean coast I came across this focaccia recipe, which I'd like to share with you all. I also met an elderly lady called Teresa, who told me her top three tips for making the perfect focaccia: always use the best extra virgin olive oil you can afford; work the dough in a warm environment, otherwise it won't rise properly; and the oven temperature must remain constant – if the oven is allowed to cool down, the focaccia will lose its soft texture.

Serves 8

500g strong white flour, plus extra for dusting
1 x 7g sachet of fast-action (easy-blend)
  dried yeast
2 teaspoons salt
4 tablespoons extra virgin olive oil, plus extra
  for greasing and brushing

For the topping
2 tablespoons extra virgin olive oil
10 fresh yellow cherry tomatoes
10 fresh red cherry tomatoes
100g pitted black olives, drained
3 tablespoons capers, drained
Large pinch of sea salt flakes
3 tablespoons shop-bought red, sun-dried
  tomato pesto

1] Place the flour in a large bowl. Add the yeast to one side of the bowl and the salt to the other. Make a well in the centre and add 3 tablespoons of the oil then gradually pour in 300ml warm water. Mix using the handle of a wooden spoon.

2] Tip out the dough onto a lightly floured surface and knead for about 10 minutes or until smooth and elastic, adding a little more flour if it's really sticky. Shape the dough into a round and place in a large oiled bowl. Brush the top with a little oil. Cover with cling film and leave in a warm place for 1 hour or until doubled in size. Grease a large baking sheet with a little oil and set aside.

3] Turn out the dough onto a lightly floured surface. Knead just 3 or 4 times to knock out some of the air. Transfer to the oiled baking sheet. Using your fingertips, push the dough to a rectangle about 30 x 24cm and 2–3 cm thick. Brush with the remaining tablespoon of oil, cover with a tea towel and leave to rise for a further 40 minutes or until doubled in size. Preheat the oven to 200°C/ gas mark 6.

4] Remove the tea towel and press your fingertips into the dough to create indentations. Drizzle over most of the oil for the topping. Press the tomatoes into the indentations, scatter over the olives and capers and sprinkle with the sea salt. Brush with the remaining oil. Bake for 20 minutes or until golden brown. Dot the top with the red pesto and transfer to a wire rack to cool slightly. Serve warm.

FOCACCIA STUFFED WITH GORGONZOLA, OLIVES, GARLIC & ROSEMARY

FOCACCIA RIPIENA DI GORGONZOLA, OLIVE, AGLIO E ROSMARINO

This is the number one bestselling bread in my restaurants. It looks fantastic, fills the kitchen with wonderful smells when it's baking, and the combined flavours of the melting Gorgonzola cheese and Leccino olives pack a huge punch. It's perfect for when you have guests. Serve with a glass or two of prosecco.

Serves 6

350g strong white flour, plus extra for dusting
5g fast-action (easy-blend) dried yeast
1 teaspoon salt
½ teaspoon caster sugar
6 tablespoons extra virgin olive oil, plus extra for greasing and brushing
1 tablespoon chopped fresh rosemary

For the filling
250g Gorgonzola cheese, cut into small cubes
150g black olives (preferably Leccino), drained and halved
2 garlic cloves, peeled and finely sliced
3 tablespoons chopped fresh flat-leaf parsley
1 teaspoon freshly ground black pepper

1] Place the flour in a large bowl. Add the yeast to one side of the bowl and the salt and sugar to the other. Make a well in the centre and add 3 tablespoons of the oil then gradually pour in 200ml warm water. Mix together using the handle of a wooden spoon to create a soft, sticky dough.

2] Knead the dough on a lightly floured surface for about 10 minutes until smooth and elastic. Shape into a round and transfer to a large, oiled bowl. Brush the top with a little oil, cover with cling film and leave in a warm place for 1 hour or until doubled in size. Grease a large baking sheet with a little oil and set aside.

3] Turn out the dough onto a lightly floured surface and knead just 3 or 4 times to knock out the air. Roll out the dough to a rectangle about 30 x 24cm. Cover with a tea towel and leave to rest for 10 minutes.

4] Scatter the Gorgonzola, olives, garlic and parsley over the dough, leaving a 1cm border clear all around. Sprinkle over the black pepper.

5] Starting from the shorter side, roll up the dough like a Swiss roll. Tuck the side edges under to seal. Transfer the roll, seam-side down, to the oiled baking sheet. Cover with a tea towel and leave to rest for 30 minutes in a warm place. Preheat the oven to 200°C/gas mark 6.

6] Brush the surface of the focaccia with the remaining 3 tablespoons of oil and prick holes all over the bread using a fork. Sprinkle over the rosemary. Bake for 35 minutes or until golden brown. Transfer to a wire rack to cool slightly. Slice and serve warm.

OLIVE & FENNEL SEED CIABATTA

CIABATTA CON OLIVE E FINOCCHIETTO

This long, flattish bread takes its name from the Italian word for slipper, which it's thought to resemble. Note that the 'starter' (known in Italy as the *biga*) needs to be made a day ahead and left to rest overnight.

Makes 4
small
loaves

10g fresh yeast
450g strong white flour, plus extra for dusting
1 teaspoon salt
50ml extra virgin olive oil, plus extra for
  greasing
180g pitted black olives (preferably Leccino),
  drained and quartered
1 tablespoon fennel seeds, crushed

For the starter
5g fresh yeast
350g strong white flour
Olive oil, for greasing

1] To prepare the starter, place the yeast and 180ml warm water in a large bowl. When the yeast has dissolved, add the flour and stir to combine for 5 minutes to form a rough dough. Grease the inside of another large bowl with a little oil and put in the dough. Cover with cling film and leave overnight (ideally for about 20 hours) in a warm, draught-free place.

2] The next day, place the 10g yeast and 340ml warm water in a large bowl. When the yeast has dissolved, add the flour and the starter. Add the salt and pour over the olive oil. Mix thoroughly. Add the olives and fennel seeds and mix until well combined. Transfer the dough to a lightly floured surface and knead for about 10 minutes or until smooth. Place the dough in a large, oiled bowl, cover with cling film and leave to rise in a warm place for 1½–2 hours or until doubled in size.

3] Turn out the dough onto a floured surface and sprinkle over a little flour. Gently press the dough to flatten to a 2cm-thick rectangle, then cut into 4 equal-sized strips. Take one strip of dough, fold one short side of it into the middle, then bring the other side over to meet it. Press down to seal. Fold in half lengthways and press to seal the edges to create a long shape. Repeat with the remaining dough.

4] Cover a tray with a tea towel and sprinkle it with flour. Place the 4 loaves on the tea towel, cover with another tea towel and leave to rest in a warm place for 40 minutes. Preheat the oven to 220°C/gas mark 7. Dust a large baking sheet with flour and lay the loaves on the sheet, spaced apart and with the folded sides down. Gently stretch the dough to create the characteristic 'slipper' shape.

5] Spray the inside of the oven with water or splash a little water using your fingertips. Bake the loaves for 20–22 minutes or until golden brown. Transfer to a wire rack to cool slightly. Serve warm.

In Italy we really celebrate our vegetables and they're often the main attraction of a meal rather than just an accompaniment to meat or fish, especially in the south. Our markets are packed full of wonderful produce and you'll only find vegetables in season, as they're so much fresher and more flavourful. In this chapter I've chosen a wide range of different recipes, many of which are quite unusual and you may not have tried before. They include various salads, vegetables to serve as part of a mixed antipasti selection, finger food, accompaniments and more substantial main course dishes. *Buon appetito!*

VEGETABLES

CAPRESE SALAD

ROASTED ASPARAGUS SALAD WITH RED ONIONS

COURGETTES PRESERVED IN OIL WITH CHILLIES, GARLIC & FRESH MINT

SOUTHERN ITALIAN PICKLED VEGETABLE SALAD

POTATO & ARTICHOKE GRATIN

AUBERGINE BALLS WITH PARMESAN, GARLIC & PARSLEY

SPICY SAUTÉED MUSHROOMS WITH GARLIC & TOMATOES

COURGETTES STUFFED WITH RICOTTA & PECORINO

BAKED COURGETTES WITH MOZZARELLA & PARMESAN

CAPRESE SALAD

INSALATA ALLA CAPRESE

The last time I saw my late father was a few years ago in a restaurant on the Amalfi coast, where we both enjoyed a wonderful Caprese salad. So when I found myself on a boat sailing along the same stretch of coast recently, I made my own version of this traditional salad in his memory. Papà – I dedicate this recipe to you!

Serves 4

4 large fresh plum tomatoes (preferably San Marzano)
3 x 125g balls of buffalo mozzarella cheese, drained
2 large handfuls (about 80g) of fresh basil

4 tablespoons extra virgin olive oil, plus extra for drizzling
Coarse sea salt
Freshly ground black pepper

1] Roughly chop the tomatoes into large chunks and put on a serving plate.

2] Tear the mozzarella and basil into large pieces and add to the plate with the tomatoes.

3] Drizzle with the olive oil.

4] Grind over some salt and black pepper. Gently toss together.

5] Drizzle with a little more oil, toss again and serve.

ROASTED ASPARAGUS SALAD WITH RED ONIONS

INSALATONA DI ASPARAGI E CIPOLLE ROSSE

Asparagus has been popular in Italy since the Roman times. Usually it's boiled or steamed, or a combination of the two in a special pan, but it's also delicious roasted with garlic in a little olive oil and lemon juice. In central Italy wild asparagus grows in abundance in the countryside in spring, often in sandy soil close to the roadside. It's green, much thinner and less woody than cultivated asparagus, and full of flavour. Here I've used fine asparagus spears – the type you buy in the supermarket – and it pairs beautifully with the roasted red onions in this salad. I make it at least once a week during our family holidays in Sardinia.

Serves 4

600g fine asparagus spears, woody ends removed
1 garlic clove, peeled and crushed
1 tablespoon freshly squeezed lemon juice
4 tablespoons extra virgin olive oil
2 large red onions, peeled and cut into slices 1cm thick
140g rocket leaves
50g Parmesan cheese shavings
Salt and freshly ground black pepper

For the dressing
2 tablespoons freshly squeezed lemon juice
1 tablespoon wholegrain mustard
1 teaspoon runny honey
5 tablespoons extra virgin olive oil

1] Preheat the oven to 200°C/gas mark 6. Place the asparagus and garlic in a roasting tin, about 25 x 35cm. Spoon over the lemon juice and 2 tablespoons of the oil. Toss together. Roast for 20 minutes. Remove the tin from the oven and leave to cool slightly. Transfer the asparagus to a plate.

2] Put the onions in the same tin as you cooked the asparagus. Drizzle over the remaining 2 tablespoons of oil and toss to coat. Roast for 25 minutes, turning halfway. Leave to cool slightly.

3] To make the dressing, put the lemon juice, mustard and honey in a large bowl, gradually add the oil and whisk thoroughly until well combined. Add the asparagus and onions and toss to coat. Season with salt and pepper.

4] Scatter the rocket on a plate and arrange the asparagus and onions on top. Serve with the Parmesan shavings on the side or scattered over the salad.

COURGETTES PRESERVED IN OIL WITH CHILLIES, GARLIC & FRESH MINT

ZUCCHINE MARINATE ALLA SCAPECE

Whenever my mother visits she always brings me several jars of preserved courgettes, as she knows how much I've loved them since my childhood. They're wonderful served as part of the antipasti table, for example with Parma ham and creamy burrata cheese (made from mozzarella and cream). You do need to make them at least a couple of weeks before serving. The courgettes will last for up to 1 month in the fridge provided they're always submerged in oil. Remove from the fridge about 1 hour before serving.

Makes
500ml

12 large courgettes
75g sea salt flakes
700ml white wine vinegar
12 fresh mint leaves, roughly chopped

5 garlic cloves, peeled and halved
4 fresh, medium-hot red chillies, halved
125ml extra virgin olive oil, plus extra for
    topping up

1] Cut the courgettes in half lengthways. Using a small teaspoon, scoop out the pulp and seeds and discard. Cut each courgette half into thirds across then slice each piece into strips lengthways, about 5mm thick. Place in a large bowl and sprinkle over the salt. Using your hands, toss together. Cover with a tea towel and leave for 10 hours at room temperature (the salt will draw out the moisture).

2] Drain the courgettes and squeeze out as much water as you can with your hands. Place in a medium saucepan with the vinegar and 250ml water and bring to the boil over a high heat. Reduce the heat to medium, stir and cook for a further 5 minutes.

3] Drain thoroughly in a colander then fill the pan with water and place it on top of the courgettes (the weight of the filled pan will squeeze out more of the liquid). Leave for 20 minutes.

4] Lay the courgettes on tea towels in a single layer and so they are not touching. Cover with another tea towel and leave to dry at room temperature for 24 hours.

5] Place the courgettes in a large bowl with the mint, garlic, chillies and oil. Season with a little salt and gently toss together. Cover with a tea towel and leave to marinate at room temperature for 12 hours.

6] Sterilise a 500ml lidded glass jar (or several smaller jars) by placing in boiling water for about 10–15 minutes. Transfer the courgette mixture to the jar and pack down the contents as tightly as possible to release any air bubbles. Add extra oil to cover, if needed. Seal tightly. Refrigerate for 2 weeks before sampling.

SOUTHERN ITALIAN PICKLED VEGETABLE SALAD

VERDURE IN SALAMOIA

This pickled vegetable salad complements rich meat dishes perfectly, and it's also a great accompaniment to serve with fish. There are many variations of pickled vegetable salad recipes in southern Italy – some contain peppers or carrots, and cloves are often used in the pickling brine. This is my favourite combination of vegetables and flavourings. Plus it's a quick no-nonsense recipe, which means you can eat it pretty much straightaway.

Serves 6

1 large cauliflower (about 1kg), cut into small florets
400g purple sprouting broccoli, cut into florets and stems sliced into bite-sized pieces
200g Borettane onions in oil or brine, drained
50g sultanas
80g caper berries, drained
50ml extra virgin olive oil

For the pickling brine
1 litre white wine vinegar
50g runny honey
2 bay leaves
4 juniper berries
45g salt
4 black peppercorns

1] Put all the ingredients for the pickling brine in a medium saucepan. Add 1 litre of water. Place over a high heat and bring to the boil.

2] Reduce the heat to medium and add the cauliflower. Simmer for 6 minutes. Using a slotted spoon, lift out the cauliflower and drain in a colander. Add the broccoli to the pan and simmer for 6 minutes. Meanwhile, transfer the cauliflower to a tea towel.

3] Drain the broccoli (discard the brine) and transfer to the tea towel. Leave the vegetables for 30 minutes or until completely dry.

4] Tip the vegetables into a large bowl. Add the Borettane onions, sultanas, caper berries and oil. Gently toss together until all the vegetables are coated in the oil. Transfer to a large serving platter.

POTATO & ARTICHOKE GRATIN

TEGLIA DI PATATE E CARCIOFI GRATINATI

Artichokes are incredibly popular in Italy. They're celebrated throughout April at many food festivals, including the famous *Sagra del carciofo romanesco*, in the central region of Lazio. For this dish I cooked whole raw artichokes, but you can use a jar of chargrilled artichoke hearts in oil if you prefer, provided you drain them well. This is a great accompaniment to roasted meat and poultry.

2 lemons (1 squeezed, 1 quartered)
6 globe artichokes, about 250g each
4 tablespoons olive oil, plus extra for greasing
100g fresh white breadcrumbs
50g freshly grated Grana Padano cheese

2 garlic cloves, peeled and crushed
4 tablespoons chopped fresh flat-leaf parsley
800g Charlotte potatoes, peeled and cut into 5mm slices
Salt and freshly ground black pepper

Serves 6

1] Preheat the oven to 200°C/gas mark 6. Fill a large bowl with cold water and add the lemon juice.

2] Peel off the dark outer leaves of one of the artichokes until you reach the tender light green leaves. Using a sharp knife, cut off the top third of the artichoke and remove the stem. Trim the base to remove all traces of green. Use a teaspoon to scoop out the hairy choke from the centre of the artichoke and discard. Rub all over with one of the lemon quarters to prevent browning. Cut the heart into quarters and immediately immerse the wedges in the lemon water to prevent discoloration while you prepare the other artichokes in the same way.

3] Heat 2 tablespoons of the oil in a large saucepan over a medium heat. Drain the artichokes and add them to the pan with 130ml of cold water and some salt. Cook for 10 minutes, stirring occasionally, until tender.

4] Meanwhile, combine the breadcrumbs, Grana Padano, garlic and parsley in a medium bowl.

5] Grease a baking dish, about 20 x 28cm, with some oil. Spread half the potatoes over the bottom of the dish. Season with salt and pepper. Scatter over a quarter of the breadcrumb mixture, then half the artichokes. Repeat this stage. To finish, scatter over a quarter of the breadcrumb mixture and lay the remaining potatoes on top. Season with salt and pepper. Scatter over the remaining breadcrumb mixture and drizzle over the remaining 2 tablespoons of oil.

6] Cover with foil and bake for 30 minutes. Remove the foil and bake for a further 45 minutes or until golden brown. Serve hot.

AUBERGINE BALLS WITH PARMESAN, GARLIC & PARSLEY

POLPETTINE DI MELANZANE CON PARMIGIANO, AGLIO E PREZZEMOLO

Most recipes for aubergines come from southern Italy – particularly Calabria and Sicily – where the vegetable has been popular for a lot longer than in the north. This great recipe came from my aunty Rafilina, one of my mother's nine sisters. We used to visit her at weekends, and as we played and chatted by the lake at the bottom of her garden she would continuously supply us with home-made finger food. These aubergine balls were always my favourite – I love the contrast between their crisp coating and their warm, creamy interior.

2 aubergines (about 250g each), cut into 2cm cubes
150g fresh white breadcrumbs
50g freshly grated Parmesan cheese
3 tablespoons chopped fresh flat-leaf parsley

1 garlic clove, peeled and crushed
1 large egg, lightly beaten
50g fine dried breadcrumbs
500ml olive oil
Salt and freshly ground black pepper

Serves 4

1] Bring a large pan of salted water to the boil over a high heat. Drop in the aubergines and bring back to the boil, then reduce the heat to medium. Place a pan lid on top so the aubergine cubes are submerged. Simmer for 10 minutes then drain thoroughly in a colander or sieve. Leave to cool slightly.

2] Using the back of a wooden spoon, press the aubergine against the side of the colander or sieve to remove as much excess liquid as possible. Chop the aubergine finely, then put in a medium bowl with the fresh breadcrumbs, Parmesan, parsley and garlic. Mash with a fork to combine, mix in the egg and season with salt and pepper.

3] Tip the dried breadcrumbs onto a plate. Using your hands, roll the aubergine mixture into small balls about the size of a walnut. Carefully roll each ball in the breadcrumbs and transfer to another plate. You should end up with about 20 balls in total.

4] Heat the oil in a large non-stick frying pan over a high heat. When the oil is very hot, carefully add the balls in a single layer and fry for about 6 minutes, turning them over as they brown. You may need to fry in batches. Transfer to kitchen paper to drain for about 2 minutes then serve.

SPICY SAUTÉED MUSHROOMS WITH GARLIC & TOMATOES

FUNGHI DI BOSCO PICCANTI CON AGLIO E POMODORINI

Wild mushrooms are found throughout Italy in autumn, with the island of Elba and the wooded hills of Sila, in Calabria, being among the best places in the country to forage for them. There are well over 200 varieties, but porcini and chanterelles are certainly the most common. For this recipe you can use whatever mixed mushrooms are available. I suggest you make double quantities and toss the leftovers in pasta the following day – delicious!

900g fresh mixed wild mushrooms (porcini, chanterelle, oyster, chestnut)
4 tablespoons extra virgin olive oil
3 large garlic cloves, peeled and halved
1 tablespoon chopped fresh rosemary

1 teaspoon dried chilli flakes
1 x 400g tin of cherry tomatoes
2 tablespoons chopped fresh flat-leaf parsley
Salt

Serves 4

1] Remove any dirt from the mushrooms with a pastry brush. Cut the mushrooms into slices 5mm thick. Set aside.

2] Heat the oil in a large frying pan over a high heat. Add the garlic and rosemary and fry for 1 minute. Tip in the mushrooms, add the chilli flakes and season with salt. Fry for 10 minutes, stirring occasionally.

3] Add the tomatoes and fry for about 8 minutes. Stir in the parsley and serve hot.

COURGETTES STUFFED WITH RICOTTA & PECORINO

ZUCCHINE AL FORNO RIPIENE DI RICOTTA E PECORINO

As I was filming in Campania I found the most beautiful restaurant in Castel Volturno – a coastal town north of Naples, which has long beaches surrounded by fragrant pine forests. The restaurant is called Da Michele, and if you're ever in the area I suggest a visit. The food is simple and true to the region – hand-made pasta, stuffed home-grown vegetables and simple salads. This courgette dish is one of their most popular offerings and has been on the menu consistently for the past nine years. Serve with a tomato and onion salad dressed with extra virgin olive oil and balsamic vinegar.

Serves 6

6 medium courgettes
5 tablespoons extra virgin olive oil, plus extra for greasing
2 garlic cloves, peeled and crushed
40g fresh white breadcrumbs

3 tablespoons chopped fresh flat-leaf parsley
250g ricotta cheese, drained
50g freshly grated pecorino cheese
1 large egg, lightly beaten
Salt and freshly ground black pepper

1] Preheat the oven to 190°C/gas mark 5. Cut the courgettes in half lengthways. Using a teaspoon, carefully scoop out most of the insides. Finely chop the courgette flesh. Lay the courgette shells, cut-side up and in a single layer, on a large oiled baking sheet. Season with salt.

2] To make the stuffing, heat 3 tablespoons of the oil in a medium saucepan over a medium heat. Add the garlic and fry for 30 seconds. Add the courgette flesh and fry for 5 minutes, stirring occasionally. Tip in the breadcrumbs and fry for 3 minutes, stirring continuously.

3] Remove the pan from the heat and add the parsley, ricotta, 40g of the pecorino and the egg. Season with salt and pepper and stir to combine.

4] Fill the courgette shells with the stuffing mixture. Sprinkle over the remaining pecorino and drizzle over the remaining 2 tablespoons of oil.

5] Bake for 30 minutes or until the top is golden.

BAKED COURGETTES WITH MOZZARELLA & PARMESAN

ZUCCHINE AL FORNO CON MOZZARELLA E PARMIGIANO

This dish is extremely popular on the west coast of Italy, where it is often served as an accompaniment to chargrilled fish. The tomato sauce can be made ahead and the whole dish assembled several hours ahead of cooking. Just add on an extra 5 minutes to the cooking time if it's being cooked from cold. Serve with warm, crusty bread.

Serves 6 as a side dish, 4 as a main course

3 tablespoons extra virgin olive oil
2 large garlic cloves, peeled and halved
2 x 400g tins of chopped tomatoes
12 fresh basil leaves, roughly torn
9 large courgettes, cut lengthways into slices 5mm thick

250ml olive oil, plus extra for greasing
80g freshly grated Parmesan cheese
2 x 125g balls of mozzarella cheese, drained and cut into small cubes
Salt and freshly ground black pepper

1] Heat the extra virgin olive oil in a medium saucepan over a medium heat. Add the garlic and fry for 1 minute. Add the tomatoes, 6 basil leaves and salt. Simmer for about 15 minutes, stirring occasionally, until quite thick. Set aside and discard the garlic.

2] Put the courgettes in a colander placed over the sink and sprinkle salt between the layers (this will draw out the moisture). Leave for 15–30 minutes, then rinse in cold water to remove the salt. Drain on kitchen paper and pat dry.

3] Heat the olive oil in a large non-stick frying pan over a medium heat. Add a single layer of courgettes and fry for about 2 minutes each side or until lightly coloured. Drain on kitchen paper, laying kitchen paper between the layers to absorb excess oil. Fry and drain the remaining courgettes in batches in the same way. Set aside.

4] Preheat the oven to 200°C/gas mark 6. Grease a baking dish, about 24 x 28cm, with a little oil. Spread one third of the tomato sauce in the dish. Place half of the courgettes on top, then scatter over half each of the basil, mozzarella and the Parmesan. Season with salt and pepper. Add another one third of the tomato sauce, then arrange the remaining courgettes and remaining basil on top. Season again with salt and pepper. Spread over the remaining tomato sauce and finish with the remaining mozzarella and Parmesan.

5] Bake for 45 minutes until bubbling and golden brown.

We Italians are very proud of our desserts and there is such an amazing variety. Generally, the desserts in southern Italy are less creamy and rich than those in the north and often contain almonds, pistachios and candied fruits — all brought to the region by the Arabs, who ruled Sicily in the 9th and 10th centuries. The south is also famous for its wonderful granitas, sorbets and ice cream. I have included a range of popular desserts in this chapter, such as tiramisù, but I have also added some recipes that are less well known outside Italy, for instance baked aubergines with sweetened ricotta served with a chocolate sauce. I know it sounds really strange, but trust me on this one — it is heavenly.

DESSERTS

FRUIT & PROSECCO JELLIES WITH VANILLA CREAM

ZABAIONE WITH LIMONCELLO & STRAWBERRIES

CHOCOLATE-DIPPED STUFFED FIGS

CHOCOLATE ICE CREAM SANDWICH

BLACKBERRY SORBET

LIQUORICE SEMIFREDDO

HAZELNUT & VANILLA CAKE

CHOCOLATE, PISTACHIO & ALMOND CAKE

BAKED AUBERGINE & SWEETENED RICOTTA WITH CHOCOLATE SAUCE

TIRAMISÙ WITH AMARETTO

FRUIT & PROSECCO JELLIES WITH VANILLA CREAM

GELATINA DI FRUTTA E PROSECCO CON PANNA ALLA VANIGLIA

This is a lovely summery dessert that looks elegant and can easily be made ahead, so it's perfect for entertaining. It contains some rather special ingredients – prosecco and bergamot syrup; this delicious syrup is made from the citrus fruit bergamot, which is cultivated only in Calabria (see page 26). You might not recognise the name or even the fruit itself, but you will certainly recognise the flavour, as it's used to flavour Earl Grey tea. Bergamot syrup is difficult to find in Britain, but you can use a few drops of orange extract as a substitute, and candied orange peel instead of bergamot peel to decorate.

Serves 4

1 Granny Smith apple
Juice of 1 lemon
500ml lemonade
8 sheets of leaf gelatine
75ml bergamot syrup
220g ripe strawberries, hulled and sliced
140ml prosecco
12 small mint leaves and 40g candied
  bergamot peel to decorate

For the vanilla cream
150ml double cream
100g mascarpone cheese
Seeds of 1 vanilla pod

1] Peel, core and cut the apple into bite-sized pieces. Squeeze over the lemon juice. Set aside.

2] To make the jelly mixture, heat half the lemonade in a medium saucepan over a medium heat. When the lemonade is almost boiling, remove from the heat.

3] Meanwhile, soak the gelatine in a bowl of cold water for 4–5 minutes (no longer). Squeeze well to remove any excess moisture then stir the leaves into the hot lemonade until completely dissolved. Stir in the bergamot syrup and the remaining lemonade. Set aside to cool slightly.

4] Divide the strawberries and apple between 4 serving glasses (ideally martini glasses). Pour over the jelly mixture to cover the fruit. Top up with prosecco and stir. Cover with cling film and chill for at least 3 hours or overnight until set.

5] To make the vanilla cream, whip the cream until thick enough to just hold its shape and form soft peaks. Using a metal spoon, fold in the mascarpone and vanilla seeds until smooth. Cover and refrigerate until ready to serve.

6] Remove the jellies from the fridge 20 minutes before serving and spoon a dollop of vanilla cream over each. Decorate with mint leaves and candied bergamot peel.

ZABAIONE WITH LIMONCELLO & STRAWBERRIES

ZABAIONE AL LIMONCELLO CON FRAGOLE

Zabaione is an old Venetian dessert traditionally made with Marsala wine (or sometimes vin santo), but here I've given it a southern Italian twist by using limoncello (see page 79) – a lemon-flavoured liqueur that is produced mainly in Campania. It's made from Amalfi lemons, which are famous for their wonderful sweet flavour and fragrance and exceptionally large size (see page 78). Raspberries are equally delicious with this dessert.

200g ripe strawberries, hulled and sliced
140ml limoncello (lemon-flavoured liqueur)
80g caster sugar
6 egg yolks
Grated zest of 1 unwaxed lemon, plus extra for decoration
120ml double cream

Serves 6

1] Put the strawberries in a medium bowl with 4 tablespoons of the limoncello and 2 tablespoons of the sugar. Stir and set aside at room temperature for 1 hour, stirring every 10 minutes.

2] Meanwhile, place the egg yolks in a heatproof bowl (preferably stainless steel) with the lemon zest and remaining sugar. Whisk using a balloon whisk until pale and creamy.

3] Set the bowl over a pan of very gently simmering water. The base of the bowl should not touch the water. Add the remaining limoncello and whisk constantly until the mixture foams and thickens. This should take about 5 minutes; remember, the mixture will thicken further as it cools.

4] Fill a slightly larger bowl with iced water and set the bowl with the zabaione mixture inside it. Leave to cool completely, stirring occasionally (it should take about 25 minutes).

5] Put the cream in a medium bowl and whip until thick enough to form peaks. Gently fold a quarter of the cream into the cooled zabaione, then the remainder.

6] To serve, divide the strawberries and their juices among 6 dessert glasses and top with a large dollop of zabaione. Sprinkle over some grated lemon zest. Serve immediately.

CHOCOLATE-DIPPED STUFFED FIGS

FICHI RIPIENI E RICOPERTI DI CIOCCOLATO

Calabria is Italy's main fig-growing region, and in September the trees in the region are bursting with this wonderful fruit. There is such an abundance of figs that many are preserved, and you'll often see farmers laying out fruit to dry in the sun, sometimes on traditional reed racks (*cannizzole*) as they have done for centuries. In this recipe – a Calabrian favourite – dried figs are stuffed with almonds and candied orange peel and dipped in chocolate. It's an amazing combination. Here I've shown how to make your own candied orange peel (which can be stored in an airtight container for about six weeks), but as a shortcut you can buy it in the shops.

Serves 12

2 large oranges
550g granulated sugar
24 dried figs

48 almonds (with the skin on)
400g dark chocolate

1] First make the candied peel. Cut the oranges into 8 wedges. Remove the flesh, leaving only the skin and pith (keep the flesh for eating later). Slice each piece of peel into 3 or 4 strips, place in a small saucepan and cover with cold water.

2] Bring to the boil, then reduce the heat and simmer for 5 minutes. Drain and return the peel to the pan with 600ml cold water. Bring to the boil, then reduce the heat again and simmer for a further 30 minutes. Transfer the peel to a plate.

3] Reduce the heat to low. Add 500g of the sugar and heat gently until dissolved. Return the peel to the pan. Increase the heat slightly and simmer for 30 minutes. Remove from the heat and leave the peel to cool in the syrup.

4] Preheat the oven to 50°C or the lowest possible gas setting. Using a slotted spoon, lift out the peel and place on a wire rack set over a baking sheet (discard the syrup). Transfer to the oven for 30 minutes to dry out. Place the remaining sugar on a plate and toss the warm peel in the sugar to coat. Spread the strips on a baking sheet for 1 hour to dry at room temperature.

5] Preheat the oven to 120°C/gas mark ¼. To stuff the figs, first remove and discard the tough stems. Cut a slit about 2cm wide and 2cm deep opposite the stem end of each fig to create a pocket. Fill each with an almond and a piece of orange peel then press gently to seal. Place the figs on a baking sheet and bake for 40 minutes, turning halfway. Remove from the oven and leave to cool. Meanwhile, line a tray or baking sheet with baking parchment.

6] Break the chocolate into a large heatproof bowl and set the bowl over a saucepan of gently simmering water. The base of the bowl should not touch the

water. Heat gently until just melted (do not stir), then remove the pan from the heat and stir. Alternatively, melt the chocolate in a microwave on medium in short bursts, stirring in between.

7] Working quickly to keep the chocolate from hardening, drop a fig into the chocolate to submerge it completely, then remove and top with an almond. Transfer the fig to the lined tray or baking sheet. Repeat with the remaining figs. If the chocolate starts to harden, just melt it again over the warm water. Leave the figs to cool and the chocolate to harden. If you like, dip or partially dip any remaining candied orange peel in the chocolate and serve on the side.

CHOCOLATE ICE CREAM SANDWICH

CUCCIOLONE

Chocolate ice cream sandwiched between two cookies – what more do you need from life?! Kids love cucciolone, and in my experience they really enjoy getting involved in making them too. You can use any cookies you like for cucciolone. Here I used choc chip cookies, which worked very well. I've also tried the same recipe with peanut and caramel cookies and it was delicious.

Makes 12

10 egg yolks
150g caster sugar
2 teaspoons vanilla extract

250g chocolate spread (e.g. Nutella)
500ml double cream
24 shop-bought cookies, about 8cm diameter

1] Put the egg yolks, sugar and vanilla in a medium heatproof bowl and set the bowl over a saucepan of simmering water. Ensure the base of the bowl is not touching the water. Stir with a balloon whisk for about 5 minutes or until the sugar has dissolved and the mixture is pale, thick and creamy. Remove from the heat and gently fold in the chocolate spread in 3 stages. Leave to cool completely.

2] Pour the cream into a medium bowl and whisk until thick enough to just hold its shape and form soft peaks. Gently fold the cream into the cooled mixture in 3 stages.

3] Spoon the mixture into a 1-litre rigid freezerproof container. Cover with a lid or cling film and place in the freezer overnight to set.

4] Remove the ice cream from the freezer 5 minutes before you are ready to serve. Arrange 12 cookies on a work surface, with the flat side facing upwards.

5] Place a scoop of ice cream on each cookie then top each with a cookie placed flat-side down to make a sandwich. Gently press the top cookie to spread out the filling. Using a palette knife, smooth the side of the filled cookies.

BLACKBERRY SORBET

SORBETTO ALLE MORE

Blackberry sorbet is always my flavour of choice and brings back memories of foraging with friends when I was a little boy. We'd pick and eat our way through the bushes, and our purple-stained mouths and fingers were always a huge source of amusement – until my mum scrubbed me clean later that evening, practically scraping off the top layer of my skin in the process! This sorbet is perfect served with a chilled bottle of prosecco.

250g caster sugar
600g fresh blackberries
Juice of 2 lemons

Serves 6

1] Put the sugar in a small saucepan with 750ml water. Heat over a low heat for several minutes until the sugar has dissolved, stirring occasionally. Increase the heat to medium and bring to the boil. Boil for 1–2 minutes then remove from the heat and leave to cool.

2] Blitz the blackberries in a food processor or blender until smooth. Place a sieve over a medium bowl and push the blackberries through using the back of a wooden spoon to remove most of the seeds. Discard the seeds.

3] Tip the blackberry purée into the cooled sugar syrup and stir in the lemon juice.

4] Pour the mixture into a 2-litre shallow, rigid freezerproof container, cover and freeze for at least 4 hours or, ideally, overnight.

5] Remove the sorbet from the freezer and blitz the mixture using a food processor or blender (blitzing will break down the ice crystals). When the sorbet is smooth, put it back in the freezer for at least 4 hours or overnight.

6] About 10 minutes before serving, remove the sorbet from the freezer to soften slightly. Serve in scoops in glass dishes or glasses.

LIQUORICE SEMIFREDDO

SEMIFREDDO ALLA LIQUIRIZIA

Liquorice has been grown along the Mediterranean coastline for centuries, particularly in Calabria, where the soil and climate are ideal (see page 27). For this dessert I've used powdered liquorice root, but I've also made it with shop-bought liquorice twists and it works well too. Use 100g liquorice twists in place of the liquorice root powder and cut the twists into tiny pieces before adding them to the milk. They won't dissolve, so you'll need to blend with a hand-held blender before adding the liquorice-flavoured milk to the egg yolk and sugar mixture.

Serves 8

250ml full-fat milk
15g liquorice root powder
4 large eggs, separated

150g caster sugar
Pinch of salt
300ml double cream

1] Dampen the bottom and sides of a 1kg loaf tin using a pastry brush dipped in water then line the tin with cling film, allowing enough to overhang the sides. Set aside. Put the milk and liquorice in a medium saucepan and heat over a low to medium heat, stirring occasionally, until the powder has dissolved and the milk is hot but not yet simmering. Remove from the heat and set aside.

2] Place the egg yolks and 100g of the sugar in a medium bowl and whisk using a balloon whisk for about 5 minutes until thick and pale. Gradually add the liquorice milk to the egg yolks in a steady stream, whisking all the time. Pour the mixture back into the pan (rinse it out first so the mixture doesn't burn) and heat gently over a low to medium heat, stirring constantly for 5 minutes or until the mixture thickens and coats the back of the spoon. Pour the mixture into a heatproof bowl. Place the bowl in a larger bowl filled with iced water. Leave to cool, stirring occasionally.

3] Put the egg whites in a separate bowl, add the salt and whisk with an electric hand whisk on full speed until they form soft peaks. Add the remaining 50g sugar and whisk until firm peaks form. Set aside.

4] Pour the cream into a medium bowl and whip until thick enough to just hold its shape and form soft peaks. Set aside.

5] Remove the liquorice mixture from the water bath. Gently fold one third of the egg whites into the liquorice mixture until well blended. Fold in the remaining egg whites in two stages then the cream. Tip the mixture into the prepared loaf tin. Fold the overhanging cling film over the top and freeze for 8 hours or until set.

6] Remove the tin from the freezer 10 minutes before serving. To serve, turn out the semifreddo onto a serving plate, carefully remove the cling film and slice.

HAZELNUT & VANILLA CAKE

TORTA DI NOCCIOLE E VANIGLIA

This hazelnut and vanilla cake is perfect served with morning coffee, or you could make it more of a special-occasion dessert by cutting it in half and making a sandwich cake with a sweetened ricotta and mascarpone filling. You can also make this cake with pistachios or walnuts if you prefer and use orange zest instead of lemon zest. No flour is used, so it's completely gluten-free.

Butter for greasing
200g hazelnuts
6 medium eggs, separated
140g caster sugar

Grated zest of 1 unwaxed lemon
1 teaspoon vanilla extract
Icing sugar for dusting

Serves 8

1] Preheat the oven to 160°C/gas mark 3. Grease a deep, loose-bottomed round cake tin, 20cm diameter, with butter and line with baking parchment.

2] Grind the hazelnuts in a food processor until fine (it doesn't matter if there are a few slightly larger pieces). Set aside.

3] Put the egg whites in a medium bowl and whisk using an electric hand whisk on full speed until they form soft peaks. Gradually add half the sugar, whisking between each spoonful until stiffer peaks form. Set aside.

4] In a separate medium bowl, whisk the egg yolks and remaining sugar using a balloon whisk for about 5 minutes or until thick and pale. Stir in the lemon zest and vanilla.

5] Using a metal spoon or spatula, fold the egg yolks into the egg whites. Now gently fold the hazelnuts into the mixture in 4 stages.

6] Spoon the mixture into the prepared cake tin and spread it out evenly. Bake for 35 minutes or until well risen and the top springs back when lightly pressed.

7] Stand the tin on a cooling rack and leave the cake to cool. Just before serving, run a knife around the cake and turn it out onto a serving plate. Lightly dust with icing sugar.

CHOCOLATE, PISTACHIO & ALMOND CAKE

TORTA CAPRESE

Capri is the number one island to visit in Italy, and this is one of its fabulous specialities – torta caprese. It's a gloriously rich chocolate cake with nuts, and beautifully sums up the simplicity and elegance of this glittering island. Serve with a little glass of vin santo.

Serves 8

80g shelled pistachio nuts
100g salted butter, plus extra for greasing
250g plain dark chocolate, about 70% cocoa solids

4 large eggs, separated
160g icing sugar, plus extra for dusting
150g ground almonds
8 tablespoons mascarpone cheese

1] Put the pistachios in a medium bowl and pour over boiling water. Leave to soak for 3 minutes then drain and peel off the skin. Roughly chop the nuts. Set aside.

2] Preheat the oven to 180°C/gas mark 4. Grease a deep, loose-bottomed cake tin, 23cm diameter, with butter.

3] Break the chocolate into a large heatproof bowl and add the butter. Place the bowl over a saucepan of gently simmering water. The base of the bowl should not touch the water or the chocolate will become bitter. Heat gently until just melted (do not stir), then remove the pan from the heat and stir.

4] Put the egg yolks and icing sugar in a large bowl and whisk using a balloon whisk for about 5 minutes until fluffy and pale.

5] Put the egg whites in a medium bowl and whisk using an electric hand whisk on full speed until firm peaks form.

6] Pour the melted chocolate into the bowl with the egg yolks and sugar and mix thoroughly. Stir in the pistachios and almonds. Gently fold one third of the egg whites into the mixture using a metal spoon. Fold in the remaining egg whites in 2 stages.

7] Pour the mixture into the prepared cake tin and spread it out evenly. Bake for 30 minutes or until well risen and the top springs back when lightly pressed.

8] Stand the tin on a cooling rack and leave to rest for 10 minutes, then turn it out onto the rack and leave to cool. Just before serving lightly dust with icing sugar, then slice and serve with a tablespoon of mascarpone per person.

BAKED AUBERGINE & SWEETENED RICOTTA WITH CHOCOLATE SAUCE

MELANZANE AL CIOCCOLATO

This is traditionally served on 15 August to celebrate the Italian national holiday *Ferragosto*. Historically, this festival celebrated the end of the harvest and provided a period of rest for labourers, but more recently it has become the time Italians take a holiday and visit their families. Southern Italians love combining savoury and sweet flavours with amazing results, and this is a prime example. It may sound strange but it works incredibly well as a dessert – do try it and see.

Serves
6–8

100g plain flour
280g caster sugar, plus extra for dusting
½ teaspoon ground cinnamon
Grated zest of 2 unwaxed lemons
500ml olive oil
5 medium aubergines (about 1.4kg), peeled and
  cut lengthways into slices 1cm thick
Butter for greasing
Icing sugar for decoration

For the sweetened ricotta
50g blanched almonds
250g ricotta cheese, drained
50g caster sugar
5 amaretti biscuits, crushed
10g candied orange peel, finely chopped
  (shop-bought or see page 202)
2 large eggs, lightly beaten

For the chocolate sauce
300ml double cream
300g dark chocolate, broken into small pieces

1] Put the flour on a plate and the 280g caster sugar on another. Stir the cinnamon and lemon zest into the sugar.

2] Heat 4 tablespoons of the oil in a large non-stick frying pan over a medium heat until very hot. Lightly coat the aubergines with flour and place in the pan in a single layer. Fry for 3 minutes, then turn over and fry for 2 minutes. Drain on kitchen paper. Repeat for the remaining aubergine, working in batches and adding a little more oil each time. While the aubergine is still warm, dip each slice in the cinnamon sugar to coat on both sides. Set aside.

3] To make the sweetened ricotta, heat a small non-stick frying pan until hot. Add the almonds and dry-fry over a medium to low heat for a few minutes, stirring and shaking the pan constantly so they don't burn. Roughly chop and put into a medium bowl. Add the remaining ingredients and stir to combine. Set aside.

4] To make the chocolate sauce, heat the cream in a medium saucepan over a low heat. When hot, remove from the heat and add the chocolate. Leave for 2 minutes (without stirring) or until the chocolate has melted, then stir until smooth. Set aside.

5] Preheat the oven to 190°C/gas mark 5. Grease a baking dish, 22 x 22cm and at least 6cm high, with butter and dust with caster sugar. Line the bottom and sides of the dish with aubergine slices, allowing some overhang.

6] Spread one third of the sweetened ricotta over the aubergines, then a quarter of the chocolate sauce and top with a layer of aubergines. Repeat twice more, finishing with a layer of aubergines. Fold over the aubergine overhang to enclose the filling. Loosen the remaining chocolate sauce with a little milk, cover and refrigerate.

7] Bake the dish for 25 minutes or until golden brown and bubbling. Remove from the oven and leave to cool completely. Cover and refrigerate for at least 4 hours, or overnight.

8] Remove from the fridge 1 hour before serving. Cut into slices and place on serving plates. Gently warm the chocolate sauce in a pan over a low heat. Drizzle over the chocolate sauce and sprinkle over some icing sugar, then serve.

TIRAMISÙ WITH AMARETTO

TIRAMISÙ CON AMARETTO

Tiramisù (which translates as 'pick me up') is a modern version of a dessert first created in Tuscany, where it was known in the 19th century as 'zuppa inglese' (English soup), because of the popularity of the dessert among the English living in the region. The original dessert had a custard base, but this was later replaced with mascarpone. There are often variations in the liqueur used. Some cooks like to use a coffee liqueur (Tia Maria), while others prefer Irish cream (Baileys), strega (an Italian herbal liqueur containing saffron) or Marsala wine. Personally, I think that nothing beats the almond-flavoured liqueur amaretto.

Serves 8

350ml cold strong black coffee, preferably espresso
150ml amaretto (almond liqueur)
200ml double cream
5 medium eggs, separated

6 tablespoons caster sugar
500g mascarpone cheese
36 Savoiardi sponge fingers (ladyfingers)
Cocoa powder for dusting

1] Put the coffee in a medium bowl and stir in 4 tablespoons of the amaretto. Set aside.

2] Pour the cream into a medium bowl and whip until thick enough to just hold its shape and form soft peaks. Set aside.

3] Place the egg yolks and sugar in a large bowl and whisk using a balloon whisk for about 5 minutes until thick and pale. Add the mascarpone and beat thoroughly. Gently fold in the whipped cream and remaining amaretto.

4] Put the egg whites in a separate bowl and whisk with an electric hand whisk on full speed until they form stiff peaks. Using a metal spoon, gently fold one third of the egg whites into the mascarpone mixture until well blended. Fold in the remaining egg whites in 2 stages. Set aside.

5] Dip one of the biscuits in the coffee for 2 seconds (no longer) and place it in the bottom of a 20 x 30 x 7cm ceramic dish, with the sugar-side facing upwards. Repeat until the bottom of the dish is covered with half the biscuits.

6] Spread half the mascarpone mixture over the biscuits, then cover with another layer of the remaining biscuits dipped in coffee as previously. Spread the remaining mascarpone mixture on top and smooth the surface using a palette knife. Cover with cling film and refrigerate for 3 hours. Just before serving, remove the cling film and dust with cocoa powder.

INDEX

AUTHOR'S ACKNOWLEDGEMENTS

I am dedicating this book to Comandante Pino Spano for all the wonderful summers we spend on the island of Sardinia in Baia Caddinas. Grazie for your friendship and for looking after my family.

Thank you to everyone involved in the making of my *Gino's Italian Coastal Escape* series and book – you know who you are! Grazie xxx